FOREWORD BY STEVE BACKLUND

REVOLUTIONIZED

by

GRACE

*Experience limitless transformation
and empowerment in Christ*

D1738366

STEPHEN BELL

DEDICATIONS

I dedicate this book to my four amazing children, Jasmine, Judah, Savannah, and Scarlett. You have brought me so much laughter and constantly remind me to lighten up and enjoy the journey of life. I love each one of you so much! My victories and revelations are yours. My ceiling is your floor—each one of you will go much further than me in your own unique connection with God and expression of grace.

Jasmine – You are my bright ray of sunshine! I love your creativity, your passion to explore new things, and the way you think outside of the box. You amaze me at how sensitive you are to God speaking to you with such accuracy and creative expression. You are a courageous overcomer and a bright light of God's kindness and beauty in a darkened world.

Judah – You are a tender and mighty warrior! I love how you deeply love and care for people, and at the same time you are a giant slayer. You blow me away with how smart you are and how much you make me laugh. I love your excitement for life, how organized you are, and your passion for superheroes. You are mighty in God's presence and you will proclaim and demonstrate the gospel with compassion and power everywhere you go!

Savannah – You are my strong and determined little sweetie! I love how affectionate you are and your constant cuddles. You bring me so much joy! You are sensitive to the presence of God and a worshiper. You are a lover of God's presence. Your strength and determination mixed with your affection will lead you to have great influence. You will demonstrate both the love and the wisdom of God. You are an influencer of influencers!

Scarlett – You are a precious gift from Papa God. I love your smile and how you are so full of hope, joy, and abundant grace. You will exceed all of us in the level of favor you will walk in. You have a heart like King David and will do battle by taking the pure worship of the King to the nations. Your inheritance is extravagant!

ACKNOWLEDGEMENTS

This book would never have happened, and the revelation of truth found in it would not be as rich, without some very important people in my life. Thank you, *Jenny Bell*, my amazing and beautiful wife. You were the one who encouraged me to persevere when I got frustrated and was ready to "burn it all up." You are the most determined person I know. The journey of life with you is so fun. I love you tons! Thank you, *Angelo Jeanpierre*, for challenging me to start this book. There was no way I was going to pay you for missing a week of writing. You're next! Thank you, *Steve Backlund,* for reading a draft of this book and giving timely and wise feedback. You have influenced me with victorious thinking more than you know. Thank you, *Duke Level,* for impacting me so deeply with the revelation of the grace gospel and living in sonship. My life will never be the same. Thank you, *Dave Clowser* and *Jan Clowser,* for never giving up on me when I was navigating through the tough seasons of my life. Jan, you taught me about the heart and voice of God in intercessory prayer. Dave, you taught me so much about lightening up and having fun … even in the presence of God. Man, I needed that! Thank you, *Ahab Alhindi,* for allowing me to read the first chapter to you in person. Your feedback and the inspiration of your own book, *Limitless Intimacy,* helped me to refocus and end well. Your passion for greatness is contagious! Thank you, *Bethel Church leadership and friends,* for the revelation and encounter of the goodness and power of God. I am so indebted to you for where I am today in life and ministry.

ENDORSEMENTS

I've had the privilege of knowing Stephen Bell as a covenant friend for ten years. The book you hold is given out of the abundance of his heart. You can only give away what you have. This is an obvious truth statement, yet so many in the body of Christ share the Gospel of Grace without fully possessing it. Stephen Bell is a man who has been possessed by the Promise of the Gospel, the Spirit of Truth. The greatest grace ever given was the person of the Holy Spirit.

Revolutionized by Grace is more than just an informational book, it's a prophetic testimony that has the power to transform your life. Expect to learn, expect tears, above all expect an encounter with Grace Himself.

Richie Seltzer
Senior Leader at Imagine Church in Calgary, Alberta

Many Christians initially accept the grace of God to be saved, knowing they were unworthy of eternal life achieved by their own merits. Once saved, however, many Christians live the rest of the their lives performing for God's acceptance and approval. This lifestyle leads to continual striving, resulting in defeat and condemnation.

Revolutionized by Grace is a great book to gain foundational understanding of God's saving grace, learning how to live in the freedom of God's grace, as well as receiving an impartation of the ongoing, empowering grace to propel you into your supernatural destiny as a world changer. Stephen Bell lives these Kingdom principles out in his daily life and ministry. I would encourage you to buy his book, read it, and do it. Soon, you will find that you have similar testimonies of God's grace working in and through your life!

Kevin Dedmon, Author
The Ultimate Treasure Hunt
Firestarters

It seems grace should be one of the easiest, non-controversial topics in Christianity, but these days grace has become an issue over which saints choose to chide and divide. "Greasy grace," "license to sin," "sloppy agape," "balance between grace and truth" ... the battle goes on!

Ah, now a breath of fresh air! In *Revolutionized by Grace,* Stephen Bell shares his personal testimony with scriptural examples to show that grace is not only liberating, but transforming! Grace is not fire insurance, but the abundant, freely-offered, freely-received power from Father God Himself that transforms us into the energized, life-sharing example we always thought was just for the superstars.

Revolutionized by Grace, although packed with revelation and scriptural truth, is an easy read. Thanks, Stephen, for helping us to see that grace is not a doctrine, but a Person—Jesus!

Jim Britton
Senior Pastor at RiverSong Church in Springfield, Ohio

In this book, *Revolutionized by Grace*, Stephen Bell unpacks the profound truth that grace is more than just unmerited favor, but actually a Person who empowers us as believers to live the Christian life that Jesus modeled for us on the earth. This book is full of insight and revelation that is presented in a way that is both practical and full of hope!

As a close personal friend of Stephen, I can tell you that he is man whose passion is bringing people into the revelation of God's goodness. He walks out what it truly means to be a part of a family in the Kingdom. His heart is to see every believer living in sonship and empowered to do all of life well. Stephen is not only a talented writer and speaker, but also a visionary who is driven by seeing Heaven invade earth. His life is a testament to the miracle-working power of Grace.

As you read, you will not only see that Stephen's heart for the church is on display through creative storytelling from his own personal life with Grace, but I pray that you will encounter the Father's heart for the unlimited measure of grace He has for you. Read, encounter, receive, and be transformed!

Adam Bowling
Worship Pastor at RiverSong Church in Springfield, Ohio

$$\diamondsuit$$

Stephen Bell really captured the heart of the Father and took grace to a whole new level in *Revolutionized by Grace*. This book is a catalyst to experience grace as a lifestyle, not just a gift. It is certainly God-breathed, leading people to their true identities and God-given destinies. It is the total framework to receive grace, walk in grace, and radically be empowered by grace! What an incredible resource and gift to the body for true transformation that will lead to bold, lifestyle Christianity as Christ intended!

Aaron Simmons
Senior Leader at Upper Room Worship Center
Author of *Born For Adoption*

$$\diamondsuit$$

There are few people in my life who have challenged me in a painfully good way. Stephen is one of those people. He spells out his heart in this wise, transparent, and empowering book. He eloquently lays out the depths of grace, while cracking mindsets and unlocking truths! It will be a catalyst for your faith and freedom to walk out the Kingdom on Earth as it is in Heaven.

Nicole Simmons
Senior Leader at Upper Room Worship Center
Author of *Best Dad Ever*

$$\diamondsuit$$

I first met Stephen several years ago while ministering at his church and in the school of ministry he led. I liked him immediately due to his genuine enthusiasm for both God and people. What particularly impressed me about him, however, was when one of the students became a little out of line in wanting to "bless me." Stephen immediately stepped in and lovingly pastored the situation. I realized here is a guy who is both passionate about the presence of the Lord and also concerned about people knowing the ways of the Lord.

I see this same two-fold value throughout his book. Essentially grace is so simple, but if not taught correctly is so easily misconstrued and abused. Congratulations to Stephen for biblically addressing what God's grace is and what it is not. I like to say, "God's grace is not license to do what we want and get away with it, rather, it is the power of God which allows us to be conformed to the image and lifestyle of Christ."

Revolutionized by Grace clearly and with creativity helps us understand what this means and how God works His amazing grace in us and through us. Additionally, some of Stephen's insights are worded positively C.S. Lewis-esque. For example, "God will one day remove everything that hinders love" is a priceless one-liner in relating why those who reject Christ are, indeed, rejecting eternal life. I believe *Revolutionized by Grace* will be a real blessing to all who partake of it.

Marc A. Dupont
Mantle of Praise Ministries

❖

Over the last five years, I have had the privilege of watching my friend Stephen Bell walk out this message, which burns inside of him. What I love about Stephen is his passion to give away what he's been given from the Lord. This is more than just a book, it's revelation birthed out of personal victories, time with Jesus in the secret place, and life-changing encounters with God. God's grace is key to everything in the kingdom! Whether you've freshly started your relationship with Jesus or you have been saved for decades, the truths in this book will set you free and empower you to access the greatest gift on earth—the grace of God!

Angelo Jeanpierre
Associate Outreach Pastor, Bethel Church
Director of BSSM City Service

Wow! Revolutionized by Grace is the journey of a man who lives what he teaches. Stephen is a friend and a favorite speaker at our school of ministry, and he writes this book the way he speaks: challenging, refreshing, full of humor, and loaded with Kingdom. You can feel the freedom in every page! Grace is still amazing!

Mary Baker
Senior Leader, Zion Christian Fellowship

We have loved Stephen Bell's teaching for years as a guest speaker, and this book is a treasure. He teaches from the heart of a spiritual father and with the authenticity and humility of someone who has walked deeply with the Lord. Thank you for opening our eyes further to the realities of the New Covenant and the riches of grace. Get ready for more hunger. Get ready for more freedom. Get ready for love encounters with Jesus!

Jim Baker
Senior Leader, Zion Christian Fellowship

TABLE OF CONTENTS

◈

Section One: Grace Transforms

Section Two: Grace Empowers

FOREWORD

Through his life experiences and personal relationship with God, Stephen Bell has a powerful revelation of God's grace that is imparted through *Revolutionized by Grace*. He explains how God's grace both transforms and empowers us, and how it will cause any reader to grow in their understanding and appreciation for grace. His vulnerability in sharing his journey gives hope for others to experience great breakthrough and to walk in freedom.

This book will ignite a new passion for God and a desire to share His goodness with others. It gives powerful revelation on the abundant, brand new life by illuminating the life we have in Jesus in a brighter way. Once we receive a revelation of God's love, as Stephen has, we will want everyone to know this love that surpasses knowledge. Stephen is a man of passion, revelation, and love. He combines fresh perspectives in the Word of God with deep insights into the workings of the Holy Spirit that impact people powerfully. He gives some great examples of sharing the gospel with others, and discusses different ways God helps us in this process and speaks to us so we can bless others.

Revolutionized by Grace will help you renew your mind with truth and walk in greater levels of freedom. The questions, declarations, and activations at the end of each chapter will help you integrate what you've read into your own life in a meaningful way. Bless you on this journey of delving deeper into God's grace. Your life will never be the same!

Steve Backlund
Bethel Church, Redding, CA
Founder of Igniting Hope Ministries

INTRODUCTION

Welcome to *Revolutionized by Grace*! This is the story of how God has completely revolutionized my life through grace and the mind-renewing truth I discovered along the way. He has radically freed me from a life of striving for significance and approval. He has freed me to be His beloved and cherished son. This process of freedom came through life-changing encounters with God and the power of believing truth. What I have discovered is the grace of God is completely liberating, life transforming, empowering, and excessive in nature. What Jesus did on the cross is more than enough. The "grace of God in truth" (Colossians 1:6) transforms the way we view God, ourselves, and our purpose on this planet.

Paul the apostle says in Romans 1:3 that "The Gospel is centered in God's Son ..." (Phillips Translation). Because this glorious good news is centered in Christ, we never graduate or move on from it. He is the foundation we build upon and our inheritance to be discovered for all eternity. Christ Himself is the greatest gift to all of humanity! Paul even said to those who were already believers in Rome: "I am eager to preach the gospel to you also who are in Rome" (Romans 1:15). There is a need for believers all over the world to dive deeper into what Christ truly accomplished on the cross and the new life we have found in Him. What He has purchased with His own blood has become our birthright as His sons and daughters. All of the mysteries and treasures of God found in Jesus are to be freely discovered and experienced with simple, childlike faith. Unfortunately, many are living on crumbs because of a misunderstanding of grace, when they could be feasting at a banqueting table set for kings. The table has already been set and the invitation is to all of humanity. This is the good news we are to taste of ourselves and then proclaim to all of the world. This is the passion and purpose behind this book.

This book covers some of the pitfalls and confusion surrounding grace, but my primary goal is for every reader to be ignited with passion for Jesus and the power of the gospel to transform lives. You will be stretched in your faith to believe the simplicity and ease of this good news, and at the same time be fueled with hope and passion to share it freely with others. This is what we were saved for. We were saved into the pleasures of knowing God and making Him known with power to the world around us.

Let's go on a journey together with the Holy Spirit to discover this glorious life into which we have been saved. Such an outrageous life of abundance purchased at such a high price is worthy of our full attention and wholehearted pursuit.

This is my prayer for you as you read this book:

> *"That God, the God of our Lord Jesus Christ and the all-glorious Father, will give you spiritual wisdom and the insight to know more of Him: that you may receive that inner illumination of the spirit which will make you realize how great is the hope to which He is calling you – the magnificence and the splendor of the inheritance promised to Christians – and how tremendous is the power available to us who believe in God"* *(Ephesians 1:17–19, Phillips Translation).*

SECTION ONE

Grace Transforms

CHAPTER ONE

Getting What We Don't Deserve

Early on a Saturday morning, I was riding in the passenger seat of a stranger's car. I was getting a ride back to my grandparents' house. Earlier that morning, I had walked down that same busy road for about three miles with no shoes or shirt on. My rage fueled me as I quickly walked down the side of the road, stepping on rocks with my bare feet, but ignoring the discomfort. My anger had numbed me from acknowledging any pain! I had reached a high school baseball field and could go no further. I was falling apart internally and felt completely alone. My actions from the last 24 hours began to set in, and my emotions came bursting out like a flood. I yelled out several times in desperation for some answers to the hole I had dug myself into. I broke down and began to cry as I made my way back to the road. Weak and desperate, I decided to hitchhike because I didn't have the strength to walk the distance back. As I slowly walked down the road with my thumb out, a woman stopped to give me a ride in her car. She asked me if I was okay, or if I needed help. I shared a little bit of what was going on with me after I hopped into her car. She tried to help by relating, but nothing could remove the emptiness I was feeling. I knew I had to just bite the bullet and head back to my grandpa. I couldn't run from my dysfunction and bad choices anymore. There were many factors leading up to this meltdown. This was just one isolated event that became the straw that broke the camel's back.

The night before, I had been heavily drinking alcohol and in a rage. My ex-girlfriend went to a school dance with another guy, and we had just recently broken up. Filled with jealousy, I went on the prowl after the dance, looking for the guy she went with. Luckily for both of us, I never found him! The cops showed up because I had terrorized a neighborhood in the process of looking for him. They ended up driving me down to the police station to detain me. They told me I had enough alcohol in my system to get three people drunk. They were shocked that I was still awake or even alive for that matter. I was a mess! They ended up letting me off the hook and sent me home with some pep talks about straightening up my life. They knew my dad, and I could tell they were very concerned for me. Unfortunately, it went in one ear and out the other.

After I got out of the police station and was home at my grandparents' house, I called my ex-girlfriend and convinced her to come over early in the morning to talk. That was a big mistake! We had a terrible argument, and I completely lost it. I began to break things and destroy the apartment I was living in above my grandparents' garage. I chased her out the door and ran right into my grandfather. He tried to grab me and calm me down, and I started yelling and cursing at him. I had never done that to him before. Once I knew everything was crumbling around me, I took off walking down the road, without a shirt or shoes. I had never felt so alone and afraid as I did that day. The drive back from the ball field to my grandparents' house is like a blur in my mind, but I distinctly remember how I felt when we pulled into the driveway. It was like a huge pit was sitting in my stomach!

I thanked the woman who gave me the ride and went up to the room I was living in—the room I had just destroyed. I found my grandfather sitting on the couch, waiting for me. I thought he was going to chew into me for what I had just done. Instead, he called me over, embraced me, and just cried with me. I finally let go of my fear and allowed myself to be broken in my grandpa's arms. It took unconditional love to melt me. Rather than punishing me, he loved me in my mess. I already knew what I had done wrong; that was pretty blatant and clear. What my grandpa did went beyond just dealing with my behavior. He touched a place in my heart that was broken and desperately crying out for love and direction. At the time, I had no idea this was my first encounter with mercy and grace. I didn't get the punishment I deserved from the police or from my grandpa (mercy), and I got what I didn't deserve (grace). My grandpa gave me something priceless that I needed so badly, and yet I didn't do anything to work for it, earn it, or deserve it. He loved me unconditionally by graciously forgiving me and giving me advice and some direction for my life. I knew he really cared, so I listened and acted on it. His advice would become the catalyst to lead me to Grace Himself.

GRACE CAME TO ME IN A PERSON

Before this had all gone down, my mom moved away from Washington (where I was) with my older sister to Virginia. My sister had married a man who was in the Navy, and my mom didn't want her to be alone while her husband was working. The first year in Virginia, my mom started going to a church she liked and gave her life to Jesus for the first time.

After experiencing this new life in Christ, she began to pray for my two sisters and me. While she was praying, the Lord spoke to her and showed her that I would be the first one to get saved out of her three kids. My mom then pointed her prayer guns toward me. UH OH! Momma was praying in agreement with God. I could run, but there was no place to hide!

After my mom had shared the gospel with me, God began to introduce Himself to me through unusual and supernatural experiences. I had a significant dream in which I knew heaven and hell were real. After that, I had an encounter with one of my managers at work who I found out was a Christian. He was praying and asking God to send a young man to him to mentor, and I started coming to him with questions about God. I knew this was no coincidence.

The most dramatic experience was when I was with my friends, getting geared up to get drunk in my friend's room. He happened to have a Bible sitting on the headboard of his bed. I opened up the Bible and a flash of light physically jumped off of the pages. This was the very first time I had ever opened a Bible. God had my attention, to say the least. What sealed the deal for me was when I was reading the book of Genesis on a camping trip. I borrowed my friend's Bible (the one from which light had jumped off the pages). I came to the realization that God was real and that I needed forgiveness. I was aware of my need for Jesus. Not too long after this, I was in my room above my grandparents' garage, and I made a conscious choice to follow Jesus for the rest of my life. I got on my knees, asked God for forgiveness for all of my sins, and asked Him to live inside of me. In that moment, I was flooded with the goodness of His presence! I had never felt anything like His presence before. The weight of sin lifted off of my shoulders, and I could feel Him living on the inside of me now. I was at peace internally for the first time in my whole life. I could feel His tangible presence all around me. Nothing the world had offered me up to that point could even compare to what I was experiencing in that moment. I was changed, exhilarated, and satisfied for the first time. What I was always longing for came to me in the Person of Jesus. Grace came into my broken and sin-stained soul to make all things new, in the very room where everything seemed to cave in on me. He is a redeeming God. The emptiness I always felt was gone. I suddenly knew the questions I always had about my purpose for being alive were being answered in Jesus. He caused everything inside of me to feel alive and free. There was no going back to the emptiness I had before this dramatic encounter. I knew I was totally getting what I didn't deserve. I was getting Jesus. I was all in!

Unfortunately, like many others, I understood what I was saved out of, but it took me quite a few years to really begin to understand what I was truly saved into. I didn't have a clue about grace transforming and empowering me to live victoriously. I didn't know I could tap into that limitless supply, so I began to rely upon myself to follow Jesus. This quickly became a horrible lifestyle of performance that Jesus had to rescue me out of.

THE CHALLENGING YEARS

The truth is we are not defined by our past experience. We are defined by God. I am going to share this challenging part of my life in hope that some who can relate to it will begin their personal journey into the freedom of grace. This is exactly what I needed, and still need, to be reminded of often.

When I got saved, I quickly had the mindset that I had to work hard to earn God's love and get His approval. I put so much pressure on myself and had a very low self-esteem. Sadly, I was taught in the church that grace saved me out of hell, but now I owed God my performance and effort to live holy for Him. I attempted this and lived up and down emotionally as a young Christian for many years. Living "up" when I felt like I was performing to my expectations of a committed follower of Jesus, and "down" when I thought I was falling short of that standard. This made relating to God and others very strained at times.

I had a wrong view of God and what He expected from me, but more than that, I had even worse views of myself. I didn't understand God's love and acceptance, and I was thinking and behaving as an orphan rather than an adopted and cherished son. Being motivated by love was not an option for me because I always had something to prove to myself and to the people around me. I had to be more sacrificial, pray harder, lead more people to Jesus, and know the Bible more than everyone around me. I was steeped in performance and spiritual pride! If I didn't live up to this standard I put on myself, I would crash into self-pity and a deep sense of failure. This became a vicious cycle of either trying really hard and striving for significance, or giving up and feeling like a failure. Motivated by fear, I would put this standard on others and became very disappointed with them when they didn't hit the mark of spirituality I considered pleasing to God. Despite my severe ups and downs with myself and others, I still had life-changing encounters with God.

In fact, I saw many of my family members brought to salvation in Jesus during this time. My Father in heaven was obviously committed to seeing me come into the glorious freedom of being His son. I am so thankful He celebrates progress and every little victory rather than demanding perfection. He is a good Father.

One thing that hindered me internally was the fact that I primarily got saved through the fear of going to hell and the fear of the end days. I was told that Jesus was returning to the earth in the year 2000, and I would go to hell if I did not receive Him into my heart. I was taught about the book of Revelation and the great tribulation before I even got saved. Wow! It took me quite a few years to understand that fear is not a good motivator to come to Jesus, or to live for Him for that matter. If fear got me in, it would take fear to keep me in! This would not have been a good plan.

Another problem that led me right into this vicious up-and-down cycle was the belief that sin is more powerful than Christ's redemptive work. I was under the impression that my one goal in life as a follower of Jesus was to work really, really hard at not sinning because sin is offensive to God. I believed God was afraid of my sin, and others in the church had this same mindset. As a result, "operation no sin" was in effect. I was completely relying upon my own willpower to deal with my sin issues rather than simply believing and resting in what Christ had already accomplished. I was striving and sacrificing for the victory that Jesus had already won on my behalf on the cross. I had no understanding of the amazing good news that the power of sin had been done away with through Christ's sacrifice. I was desperate for truth that would set me free. The solution for me was simply believing truth. I needed to think differently but this seemed too good to be true. Could life in Christ actually be this good? Somehow I thought I needed to work hard to get what Jesus already purchased with His blood. I understood forgiveness and what I had been saved out of, but no one was telling me about the victorious and abundant life I had been saved into. I quickly became a legalist who relied upon my ability to obey God for holiness. Little did I know that the law of the Old Covenant demands my performance, but it cannot provide the empowerment to live a victorious and joy-filled life!

> "Not that we are sufficient in ourselves to claim anything as coming from us, but our sufficiency is from God; who has made us sufficient to be ministers of a New Covenant, not of the letter [ten commandments – the law] but of the Spirit. For the letter [the law] kills, but the Spirit gives life" (2 Corinthians 3:6–7).

For me, it was a process to come out of relying on my own willpower and performance and into the abundant supply of His grace. This transformation happened for me through experiencing God's pure goodness and by the renewing of my mind. Jesus said, "You will know the truth and the truth will set you free" (John 8:32). I had to begin to love truth and believe it. The more revelation I received of this gospel of grace and my identity as God's son, the more freedom I began to live in. This did not happen overnight for me. For some it has been a quicker process. Either way, Christ Himself is the cure. All of us are invited into this glorious freedom that was paid for at such a high price. Anything less is living far below our birthright as sons and daughters of God.

GOOD NEWS

What I discovered is the word "gospel" in the original Greek language means "good news" or "glad tidings." This is not just a nice concept to somehow hook people into being a Christian so they can work really hard at changing their behavior and being a good person. What God has to offer us is an invitation into a completely new life in Christ, which produces pure gladness of heart. This new life was entirely purchased by the sacrifice of God's Son on the cross. It cannot be obtained by our own effort and self-will. We simply receive this good news and walk in it by faith—childlike faith.

The truth of the matter is God really is good. He is not interested in us performing for Him through good behavior. If performance through good deeds and behavior is what God is looking for, then Jesus died for nothing. We have been saved into something so glorious that it really does take childlike faith to believe it. God offers all of humanity a brand new life and a fresh start.

He never intended on fixing your old life of sin. He crucified it with Christ on the cross. Your old life of sin is dead! This is the scandal of grace. You completely get what you don't deserve. We can't fix what is broken and we can't earn this new life found only in God's Son. Jesus has always been the solution. This is rooted in the pure goodness of God. He cannot be anything other than good. He doesn't have mean streaks, hidden motives, or character flaws.

How we view God affects every other aspect of our lives. It affects the way we view ourselves, others, our circumstances, and issues in the world around us. Everything in our lives must be built upon this one foundational belief: God is good 100% of the time. Living in God's limitless grace is rooted in this one core belief.

Consider part of Adam Clark's definition of God in his commentary of the Bible, concerning Genesis 1:1.

> *"Many attempts have been made to define the term God: as to the word itself, it is pure Anglo-Saxon, and among our ancestors signified, not only the Divine Being, now commonly designated by the word, but also good; as in their apprehensions it appeared that God and good were correlative terms; and when they thought or spoke of Him, they were doubtless led from the word itself to consider Him as The Good Being, a fountain of infinite benevolence and beneficence toward His creatures."*

> *"The eternal, independent, and self-existent Being: the Being whose purposes and actions spring from Himself, without foreign motive or influence: He who is absolute in dominion; the most pure, the most simple, and most spiritual of all essences; infinitely benevolent, beneficent, true, and holy: the cause of all being, the upholder of all things; infinitely happy, because infinitely perfect; and eternally self-sufficient, needing nothing that He has made ..."*

Could it be true that we cannot separate the word "God" from the word "good?" That God really is "infinitely happy" and "The Good Being?" I say yes. I say this with confidence because not only have I discovered the truth of this happy news in the Scriptures, but I have also experienced it first-hand and tasted the pure joy of it found in Jesus. Christ Himself is at the center of this good news, and in Him we find "pleasures forevermore" (Psalm 16:11).

THE SCANDAL OF GRACE

The truth that God is a continual fountain of pure goodness toward all of humanity seems too good to be true, simply because we did not earn, work for, or deserve it in any way. This is why grace is so scandalous and sometimes a hard pill to swallow for some. The gospel begins with the truth that we completely receive a free gift we absolutely do not deserve. The Father of lights extends His mercy and grace to us purely based upon the sacrifice of His Son. Mercy is not getting what I deserve and grace is getting what I don't deserve. All of us deserve punishment for our sin, and yet we find forgiveness and an abundant life instead.

This is not based on any of our works but purely on the works of Christ. We have been rescued from darkness and our new home is in the kingdom of light.

> "For we must never forget that He rescued us from the power of darkness, and reestablished us in the kingdom of His beloved Son, that is, in the kingdom of light. For it is by His Son alone that we have been redeemed and have had our sins forgiven" (Colossians 1:13–14, Phillips Translation).

Grace completely revolutionizes us. It's a radical change from one kingdom to another—from a slave-driving taskmaster to a really good King. It is a complete internal takeover that leads us instantly out of bondage and into true freedom. You and I could not have thought up or worked out in our best efforts what God accomplished for us through the death and resurrection of His Son. All that's required is that we believe. Behavior and actions always come out of what we believe.

I had to come to the realization that it wasn't me trying to convince God He was good, but it was Him trying to convince me! God was not demanding me to change and manage my behavior to somehow please Him with my performance. No, it was in the truth of God's extravagant love and grace that I realized I had already received a new nature. I could now live in victory over sin and with overflowing joy. It's this glad news that I so desperately needed in my own life that He invites all of humanity into. It's the glad news of his transforming and empowering grace!

QUESTIONS:

- Have you ever felt like you needed to perform or strive to get God's attention or approval? What was the result of that? What is God doing to renew your mind and bring you into freedom?
- What has your experience been with God as "infinitely happy"? Do you view Him as being good 100% of the time toward you? Does this truth change the way you relate to Him?

DECLARATIONS:

- I don't have to earn my Father's love. I am free to live from His love and approval!
- I am a recipient of the extravagant grace of God. I receive what I don't deserve!
- God is a continual and overflowing fountain of pure goodness. God lives in me!

ACTIVATIONS:

- Thankfulness is the greatest response to grace. Take some time to thank God for the freedom He has already brought you into and the greater levels of freedom you will be experiencing. Celebrate what He is doing rather than focusing on what isn't happening. Starting your day with intentional thankfulness is vital to victorious living.
- Take some time to be still in God's presence and meditate on God as a fountain of pure goodness. He is the One pursuing your heart. Give Him permission to pour out His goodness on you and see what happens.
- Continue with the declarations and activations at the end of each chapter. These tools will assist you to walk in greater levels of freedom.

CHAPTER TWO

The Divine Exchange

It was important for me to first look to the cross to grasp the freedom God created me to live in. I needed a better understanding of what He did on my behalf. What I discovered is Jesus didn't just die for me, He died as me in my place. To say that He just died for us is a major understatement! The result of Him dying for us is the forgiveness of our sins. This is amazing in and of itself. We are now justified as if we never sinned. We are declared not guilty in the courtroom of heaven. This is something to celebrate! The result of Him dying as us in our place is a completely transformed life. He didn't die to just let us off the hook from our acts of sin. He died as you and me to destroy the very sin nature residing inside of us that drove us to rebel against God. He died to rewrite our history and to make us new. He died to reconcile the whole world to the Father and to bring us into harmony with heaven. The Greek verb for reconciled is actually "exchanged." He literally became sin as He took our place of punishment so we could become the righteousness of God.

"For He made Him who knew no sin to be sin for us, that we might become the righteousness of God in Him" (2 Corinthians 5:21).

Jesus got our punishment and in exchange we get His righteousness. We get His nature. This is the divine exchange! This exchange is rooted in the core belief that God is a redeeming God. There is nothing in our lives or our past that the cross cannot handle.

FREEDOM FROM SHAME

The iniquity of us all was laid upon Jesus (Isaiah 53). What is iniquity? It is everything that resulted from the fall—the condition and the result of the sinful nature that was residing in us. This is primarily speaking of guilt, shame, and our need for punishment. He not only took upon Himself the sins of the whole world, but also the result of our sins. He paid for the very things that plague humanity apart from Christ—shame, guilt, punishment, sorrow (depression), sickness, disease, poverty, etc. Guilt comes from knowing we have done something wrong. This can be positive and negative. Guilt is initially positive when we feel bad about a decision that negatively affects our relationship with God or others. It is negative if that sense of guilt remains after we have asked for forgiveness and made things right in our relationships.

Shame is entirely different and it is never positive. Shame is not just feeling bad about something we have done wrong, it's the strong sense of feeling bad about who we are. Shame is believing the lie that there is something very bad about who we are as a person.

In my experience, shame is usually connected to isolated events that were very negative or destructive in nature. Shame leads to fear and isolation, and it ultimately works to break down connection in relationships. Jesus came to remove the sense of guilt through the forgiveness of our sins and He also came to remove our shame through the power of acceptance. He restores the dignity of our identity. He wants us to feel good about who we are in Him. This happens through the process of experiencing and believing the extravagant love and acceptance God has for us. This is the power and the beauty of the divine exchange—Jesus became our sin and shame so we could be acquitted and live free. You are no longer a slave, and you are no longer under the power of shame! We were co-crucified with

Christ, and the result is all things are restored and made new. He came to restore you back to the pinnacle, the high place of affectionate union and partnership with God. Jesus alone is the cure for our iniquity. He alone destroyed the very things that brought distance and separation between our Papa God and us.

THE CROSS IS ENOUGH

I lived in the land of shame for many years for one specific reason: I didn't understand the power of what Christ fully accomplished on the cross. I didn't understand the power of God's acceptance. As a result, I was steeped in performance (as I explained in the first chapter). Shame fuels a performance driven life. It becomes a drive to prove our worth rather than living from the Father's acceptance. If we feel bad about who we are, then we will try to earn what Jesus already paid for on the cross. This is a trap to keep us in bondage. God's love and acceptance is the bondage breaker!

When Jesus said, "It is finished" on the cross, He was not exaggerating. He really meant it. He destroyed the power of sin and its destructive effect on humanity once and for all (Hebrews 7:26–27, 1 John 2:1–2). The cross truly is enough!

In doing so, Christ Himself became our salvation and the salvation for the whole world. He alone worked salvation in our place and on our behalf so we can now live in wholeness in our spirit, soul, and body. When Christ lives on the inside of us by faith, we receive things so glorious that our minds cannot fully comprehend.

We actually need help from the Holy Spirit to reveal to us the things that were prepared for us before the foundation of the world—the mysteries of God freely given to us through the revelation of Christ.

> *"Eye has not seen, nor ear heard, nor have entered into the heart of man the things which God has prepared for those who love Him. But God has revealed them to us through His Spirit. For the Spirit searches all things, yes, the deep things of God"* (1 Corinthians 2:9–10).

The Spirit is the One who happily reveals to us what we cannot comprehend on our own. He reveals what is freely ours in Christ. This is a window into the pure goodness of God and how extravagantly gracious He is toward us. He sent His cherished Son to the earth to taste death so we could live in abundant life. He gave us His very best! If you are convinced that you don't deserve it, you are right! We need to get over the fact that we don't deserve it and realize our own performing to earn what Christ paid for could not be accomplished in a hundred lifetimes. Jesus alone is the only sacrifice pleasing to the Father for our redemption and life of victory. What God offers us is pure joy and unlimited, overcoming grace.

PERSONAL REVELATION OF THE CROSS

I was in a time of prayer one evening in my dorm room at Youth With a Mission (YWAM) in Northern California. As I was praying, I had a clear vision of Jesus on the cross. It was an inner vision, almost like a movie unfolding in my mind. I could see Jesus up close in agony, hanging on the cross with His blood running down His battered body. This encounter was very personal for me. In that moment, more than any other time in my life, I knew He didn't just die for the whole world but He died for me—as me. His blood was shed in my place and I was completely undone by His overwhelming love. He was healing and restoring me deeply on the inside as an "ugly" cry came out of me.

This lasted for several minutes as He was uprooting shame and abandonment. This experience was one of the starting points of true freedom in my life. It all started with me humbling myself and acknowledging the truth that Jesus fully got what I deserved on the cross. This was pure love staring me in the face. It has a life-altering effect if it is fully embraced and digested! From this revelation, life becomes a journey of fully discovering and receiving what we absolutely don't deserve—what we cannot earn or pay for. He redeems all things! It's purely because we are loved. God did not send His Son to die in our place only to manipulate us into somehow paying Him back with good Christian behavior. With God, there are no strings attached in this outrageous exchange. He became our sin and took our punishment, and we get His abundant life and His nature infused into us. He was bruised and whipped, and we get healed because of this.

The whole world is longing for a gospel that is more powerful than the problem of sin and death. What Christ accomplished on the cross is more than enough for the whole world. The love of God trumps the greatest of sins. I was driving in my car one day, thinking about an isolated event in my past. The more I meditated on it, the more I started to feel shame setting in. The devil likes to remind us of our past because he knows the effects of shame. In that moment, I heard the voice of my Father. He said, "My love trumps your greatest sin!" His words instantly broke every sense of shame and reminded me of the truth of this divine exchange. He reminded me that my past does not define who I am—He does. For one woman in the Bible, this exchange became a reality because of her simple faith.

HER "UNCLEANESS" ... HIS POWER TO HEAL AND RESTORE

"A woman who had suffered a condition of hemorrhaging for twelve years – a long succession of physicians had treated her, and treated her badly, taking all her money and leaving her worse off than before – had heard about Jesus. She slipped in from behind and touched His robe. She was thinking to herself, 'If I can put a finger on His robe, I can get well.' The moment she did it, the flow of blood dried up. She could feel the change and knew her plague was over and done with. At the same moment, Jesus felt energy (power) discharging from Him. He turned around to the crowd and asked, 'Who touched My robe?' His disciples said, 'What are You talking about? With this crowd pushing and jostling You, You're asking, "Who touched Me?" Dozens have touched You!' But He went on asking, looking around to see who had done it. The woman, knowing what had happened, knowing she was the one, stepped up in fear and trembling, knelt before Him, and gave Him the whole story. Jesus said to her, 'Daughter, you took a risk of faith, and now you're healed and whole. Live well, live blessed! Be healed of your plague'" (Mark 5:25–34 MSG).

This story is amazing because of this woman's faith and because of the response Jesus gave her when He found out it was her who touched Him. In those days, it was actually punishable for her to touch anyone because she was considered unclean. The mindset was that if she touched another person, she would make them unclean. It was also counter-cultural for her as a woman to approach a Rabbi (a teacher) and not only touch him, but simply to address him. This explains why she was terrified to admit to Jesus it was her who touched Him. She lived in a culture of punishment based on the law of Moses. Jesus came full of grace and truth right into this culture of punishment and gave this woman her dignity back. Grace not only forgives but also has the power to transform!

Jesus took her affliction, and in exchange she received freedom and wholeness in her body. He freed her from 12 years of a torment. This was an expression of the Father's perfect love. She simply thought about what she believed and then acted upon it. Her actions necessitated huge risks, both culturally and in her faith, and Jesus honored her for it. As a result, He restored her value and dignity as a daughter. She was culturally an outcast—an untouchable. He took her shame, and in exchange she received acceptance and identity. This is what Jesus does. This is what we can expect for anyone who comes to Him with simple, childlike faith. Faith that doesn't concern itself with what the masses are saying and doing.

This is the beautiful story of the good news of Jesus and what happens when someone comes into contact with Him. All things are made new! She didn't do some righteous act to earn her healing. She got it for free simply by believing that Jesus is who He says He is and does what He says He'll do. He truly is good.

CHRIST OUR SALVATION

The amazing truth is we get Jesus Himself in this exchange. Papa God takes our sin nature that separates us and gives us His best. He gives us His Son. Salvation is not a doctrine to adhere to and just agree with; it is the greatest gift to be received. Salvation is a Person (Isaiah 12:1–6). We actually receive Christ Himself into our lives and become completely transformed into a new creation.

He is the greatest gift to all of humanity! In fact, Paul tells us about the mystery that God kept hidden from ages and generations past: "Christ in you, the hope of glory" (Colossians 1:26–27). Christ Himself has become the very life that sustains us. We actually have the solution to all of the world's problems residing on the inside of us. We are the light of the world that shines into every circumstance. Salvation resides within us in the Person of Jesus and we get to enjoy Him for eternity.

Isaiah chapter 12 tells us we can "draw water from the wells of salvation." Notice the word "wells" is plural and not singular. What are these wells we are to draw from? I discovered this mystery by simply studying the definitions of the word "salvation" in the Hebrew and Greek. Here's what I found:

> **Salvation:** (Isaiah 12:3) Hebrew word "yeshuwah" – deliverance, aid, victory, prosperity, health, help(-ing), save, saving, welfare. Root word "yasha" – to be open, wide or free, to be safe, to be free, avenging, defend, deliver, help, preserve, rescue, get victory.

> **Saved:** (Mark 16:16) Greek word "sozo" – to save, deliver or protect, heal, preserve, do well and to make whole and complete in your spirit and soul and body presently and always.

These are the wells we have access to draw from with joy. We can draw from these wells at any time because all of these realities are found in Christ, and Christ is in us. The truth that we can joyfully experience all that Christ is and all that He has to offer us is a great blessing. There is fullness of joy in His presence! (Psalm 16:11). This is our birthright and the very life we get to share with those around us. We get Christ, and we have the privilege of giving the very life of Christ away to the world.

We have been given an invitation to:

> *"Come, everyone who thirsts, come to the water; and he who has no money, come, buy and eat! Come; buy wine and milk without money and without price. Why do you spend your*

money for that which is not bread, and your labor for that which does not satisfy? Listen diligently to Me, and eat what is good, and delight yourselves in rich food. Incline your ear, and come to Me; hear, that your soul may live ..." (Isaiah 55:1–3a).

This invitation can only be fulfilled in Jesus. Why? Because there is only one way in which we can buy something without any money—if it has already been paid for in full. We have endless credit in our favor because of the blood of Jesus! This is not in any way a license to have an attitude of entitlement. On the contrary, we are to come with a heart full of gratitude as we access and receive what He has promised. The Lord Himself has set the table, and He says, "Come, everyone who [hungers and] thirsts!"

QUESTIONS:

- How have you already experienced the divine exchange in your life? Are there currently any specific areas of your life that you would like to exchange for the healing and freedom Jesus provides?
- How have you experienced joy in your salvation? On a scale of 1–10, 10 being the highest, what would you say your joy level is? How can you increase your joy in Him?

DECLARATIONS:

- Jesus died as me in my place. I have been made the righteousness of God in Christ!
- Christ is my salvation. All the wells of salvation are my birthright as a child of God!
- I am designed to overflow with joy!

ACTIVATIONS:

- Imagine yourself in the very place the woman with the issue of blood was in. You are reaching out to touch the hem of Jesus' robe. What is He speaking to you as you reach out to Him? Receive His healing and allow Him to speak to you in a way that restores your dignity and value.
- Meditate (fill your mind) on the Hebrew and Greek meanings of salvation listed in this chapter. Ask God to renew your mind with this gold mine of truth. "Joyfully pull up buckets of water from the wells of salvation. And as you do it give thanks to God" (Isaiah 12:3 MSG). Access these wells with childlike faith—it is your Father's good pleasure to give them to you!

CHAPTER THREE

Pursued by Love

For many years, I thought my connection with God was completely dependent upon me pursuing Him. I would strive and perform for this daily. What I discovered is our pursuit is simply a response to the reality that God is the One pursuing us. This truth changes everything because it empowers us to begin to live from love and approval rather than for it. The truth is everything good originates with God. This is the nature of grace. He is the One who made the first step to restoring the relationship with His treasured creation. He came out of heaven and into our world to reveal His extravagant love and kindness toward us through His Son. He didn't come to condemn us or even count our sins against us. He came to forgive us and restore us to relationship. He came to lavish His outrageous love upon all of humanity.

"We love because he first loved us" (1 John 4:19).

This is such a profound truth that is so important for us to have settled in our hearts and minds. The reality is loving God and loving others does not originate with us. This kind of love being sustained in our lives can only be produced as we choose to receive and to believe the love God first had for us (1 John 4:16).

THE TWO GREAT COMMANDMENTS

Let's take a look at the two greatest commandments of the Old Covenant, which according to Jesus sum up all of the law and the prophets: "You shall love the Lord your God with all your heart and with all your soul and with all your mind" (Matthew 22:37) and "You shall love your neighbor as yourself" (Matthew 22:39). This is absolutely true, yet many have turned these two commandments into the new "do it yourself" law of the Christian faith in an attempt to prove our devotion to God. Believe me, I personally know this thought process very well! These two commandments, like the whole of the law of Moses, are impossible to produce apart from the empowering grace of God in our lives. Jesus actually gave His disciples a new commandment knowing we could not fulfill these two commandments with our own willpower. "Love one another just as I have loved you" (John 13:34–35). This changed everything. This new commandment Jesus gave starts with receiving God's love and then empowers us to love others. The key to living a life of love is first found in receiving the Father's love.

When you and I come to experience this abundant love God has for us, we are transformed into new creatures with the ability to radically love back. Not just with human love, but with the love of God poured into our hearts (Romans 5:5). The more we encounter His love, the more we will be filled up with "all the fullness of God" (Ephesians 3:19) to give away to each other in the family of God and to the world around us.

Every time we experience God's intense love, it actually empowers us to live out the two greatest commandments. Our love and devotion can be exhausted, but God's love is limitless. His love gives us the confidence to love Him and others without fear. We live from His generous love—from fullness.

"... that you, being rooted and grounded in love, may have strength to comprehend with all the saints what is the breadth and length and height and depth, and to know the love of

Christ that surpasses knowledge, that you may be filled with all the fullness of God" (Ephesians 3:17–19).

God is the lover of your soul and has always been the One pursuing you! Loving Him, praising Him, and serving Him is simply meant to be a response to His great love and the kindness He has shown us through His Son. If it's not, we will burn out quickly by trying to prove our love and devotion to Him. The good news is God has already proven His love and devotion to us through the cross. Our job is simply to believe it and receive it with a heart full of gratitude.

SURPRISED BY LOVE

A number of years ago, I was on staff at a YWAM training base in Chico, California. The base is back in a valley surrounded by beautiful hills on either side. Many times I would hike the trails to enjoy the beauty of the landscape and to spend alone time with God. One day, I decided I was going to hike to the top of a big hillside and have the most dramatic encounter with God I had ever experienced. I was imagining thunder and lightning or a glory cloud showing up as I strived with everything I had to the top of this hill. As I reached the top of the hill, I noticed big rocks that were split and charcoaled trees from lightning strikes. This only confirmed to me even more that I was going to have a Moses on Mt. Sinai experience and would come down from the hillside glowing from God's glory!

It's actually quite comical now that I think about it, and I am not exaggerating what my mindset was either. As I stood on top of that hill, I dramatically asked God to tell me the one thing He most wanted to speak to me in that moment. I asked with great expectation! I listened for only a few seconds and quickly heard a very quiet voice say to me, "I love you, son." To be honest, I felt deflated and a little out of sorts when I first heard that. I knew it wasn't me because I was not looking for that kind of response. I was expecting fireworks!

All of the striving and lofty expectations melted as I pondered what I just heard. There were no peels of thunder or glory clouds appearing. No open visions of chariots and fire or anything like that. Just love. Pure undiluted love from a good Father who was clearly pursuing my heart more than my great exploits. He was convincing me of something that I already had—something I thought I still had to strive and prove myself for: His unconditional love and pleasure in me as His son. Don't get me wrong. I believe in the power of dramatic encounters with God and having the boldness to accomplish great exploits for the kingdom. Our value system is not found in these things, though. Our value system is found only in the Father's outrageous love for us no matter what our occupation or circumstances are. Jesus is our greatest example of this reality. He was secure and confident as a beloved Son, whether He was working as a carpenter or moving full swing in miracles and walking on water. His value system did not come from what He was accomplishing. It came from His love relationship with His Father as a cherished, beloved Son. His value system remained the same no matter what He was doing in life. His doing came out of His being. This was the Father's invitation to me at the top of that hill. It started with me letting go of my need to prove myself and learning to receive His extravagant love and grace. This is where healing and transformation happen. The whole world needs this baptism of love.

THE VEIL IS TORN

There is nothing hindering or blocking our access to the Father. When Jesus died, the Bible tells us the veil that separated mankind from God's holy presence in the Jewish temple was "torn in two, from top to bottom" (Matthew 27:51). This veil is said to have been so thick that two horses tied to either side could not tear it apart. God Himself ripped this veil in His pursuit of our hearts. He passionately tore in two the very thing that separated us. At the cross, the Father kissed an orphaned world as He was calling us all home!

Now, through the blood of His Son, we have access to the presence of God anytime and anywhere. Even more important than this is the truth that God, the Lover of our souls, now has access to us. He can wrap His love and presence around us like a hug, anytime and anywhere.

"I will give you a new nature, and I will put a new spirit into you, I will take away your hard nature [heart] and give you a nature [heart] that can be touched" (Ezekiel 36:26 Moffatt).

God made it possible to touch your life. Wow! I will say it again and will continue to say it—the cross is enough. We no longer live for acceptance and approval. We live from acceptance and approval. We live from perfect love, not for love. God was and is and always will be the Pursuer of all humanity.

When the prodigal son turned his heart back to his father in Luke 15, he found himself overwhelmed by an unconditional love he did not expect, work for, or deserve. His thinking was not even right in turning back, but he was met with his father crashing into him with a full embrace and an affectionate kiss on his neck. Your Father is waiting to crash in on your life with a kiss of pure acceptance. Just turn your heart to Him through the lense of the cross, and make yourself at home in His loving presence. This is where you were meant to live. This is the place where your life will never be the same!

FAITH COVENANT

God has completely changed the way He interacts with humanity since the cross. Let's take a look at the difference between the covenants in a simple and non-exhaustive way. The Old Covenant is a list of laws and regulations that the Jewish people were primarily commanded not to do in order to somehow attain to God's holy standard of living. His standard of living, according to the Jewish law given to Moses, was perfection. This was attained by obedience alone and the ability to keep the rules in order to receive favor with God and receive what He had promised. The problem with this is God never desired controlled behavior based on rules and regulations. He has always desired heart connection with His people.

The law was established for good reasons, though. I will explain this in more detail in the next chapter. The New Covenant is justification by faith in Christ as if we had never sinned. We receive the promises of God completely by faith and not by performing for them through rules and regulations. This is based on an inward exchange and transformation through faith in Christ that leads us to an organic and intimate relationship with Him. We know this was and always will be God's heart because this is what God established with Abraham before the law was ever introduced. Grace and faith came before the law.

Abraham was declared righteous and obtained the promises purely by faith. He simply believed what God said to him. Instead of believing he had to perform to earn what God promised, Abraham simply lived by faith in God's ability to fulfill what He had promised. It wasn't about Abraham's pursuit of God—it was about God's pursuit of Abraham! Through this, God invited Abraham into a covenant relationship where He had his back no matter what. God still had Abraham's back even when he lied about Sarah being his sister and put Abimelech and all of his people in jeopardy of God's judgment. This is covenant.

God will always be true to His promises even when we make stupid choices out of fear. Obviously I am not condoning being irresponsible with the idea that we can do whatever we selfishly desire simply because God has our backs. This is not the case with Abraham because he made his connection with God and trust in Him the top priority. God honored His friend and had his back in a sticky situation because of the level of covenant relationship He initiated with him. Abraham didn't deserve this kindness from God because he is the one who got himself into that sticky situation in the first place. In fact, after God confronted Abimelech in a dream, Abimelech went straight to Abraham and confronted him as to why he lied. This forced Abraham to take ownership for what he did and to clean up the mess he created. Amazing! God addressed the issue with Abraham through relationship rather than punishment for what he had done. He also gave Abimelech the opportunity to repent. Here's the profound truth: We can't screw it up! God is too good and committed to us when it comes to His purpose for our lives. This is the difference between an outward appearance of keeping the rules and having good behavior versus living from the inward reality of connection with God through faith. The focus is on the greatness of the One who gives the promise, not on our efforts to obtain the promise.

LIVING FROM THE HEART

Lovers and friends of God have privileges that others don't have! A great example of this is when David was given the bread of the Presence from the temple as he was running from Saul (1 Samuel 21:1–6). This was actually breaking the rules, but David and his men were desperate and hungry. Why didn't God discipline David or maul him with a bear or something? It's because of the depth of David's relationship with God. He knew the kindness of God by experience and actually tapped into New Covenant grace. David knew God valued relationship from the heart more than obeying the rules. His faith in a good God enabled him to enjoy privileges that others didn't know were even accessible.

The New Covenant is an inward reality where we live from a transformed and God-filled heart. It's what we get to do from love, not what we cannot do based on rules and fear. Consider this quote from Steve Backlund out of his book *Victorious Mindsets*:

> "*Understanding [and experiencing] God's kindness and good-ness will cause us to want to pursue a relationship with Him that will change us from the inside out (because we will be responding from love rather than fear). This relationship will ignite us to the abundant life that Jesus promised. We will no longer be focused on performance, but rather on experiencing newer and deeper dimensions of our heart connection with God (His kindness). This will change our behavior like nothing else will.*"

We don't need to perform out of fear anymore. We can drink deep of the love and goodness of God, so much that it becomes our great pleasure to live a surrendered life to Him. Our behavior begins to change from understanding and experiencing the love and kindness of God. We were meant to live from the heart, not from a list of rules. It becomes less about my sacrifice "for God" and more about being compelled by the love of Christ at work in me. The New Covenant is an invitation into the pleasures of unbroken union with God and into partnership with Him in seeing His kingdom advanced in the earth. Knowing God intimately is our greatest privilege.

FEASTING ON GOD

"Lord, even when Your path takes me through the valley of the deepest darkness You remain close to me and lead me through it all the way. Because You are with me I have no fear of danger! Your authority is my strength and peace. The comfort of Your love takes away my fear. I'll never be lonely for You are near. You become my delicious feast even when my enemies dare to fight. You anoint me with the fragrance of Your Holy Spirit, You give me all I can drink of You until my heart overflows" (Psalm 23:4–5 TPT).

When Jesus introduced the New Covenant to His disciples, He instructed them to drink the wine, symbolizing His blood for the forgiveness of sins. He also instructed them to eat the bread, symbolizing His broken body for the healing and wholeness of the whole world. He instructs us to literally drink in what He accomplished on the cross and to feast on Him—to take God in and digest Him into every part of our being. This is God living on the inside of His people. God living with us! God Himself becomes our delicious feast and in Him we are truly satisfied. We can drink in His love and presence until our hearts are overflowing with His goodness. Think about it—God is living on the inside of you and me! It doesn't get any more intimate, satisfying, or any more spiritual than God living in us and becoming one with our spirit. (1 Corinthians 6:17) We are His inheritance and He is ours. He takes all of our sin and baggage and we get Him. This delicious feast is reserved for the surrendered lovers. We get Him, and He wants all of us. Many people ask me how they can experience more of God and see more breakthrough in their lives. My answer is simple: Delight yourself in God and take advantage of your access to what Christ already paid for with confidence. Choose to live from the truth of your Father's unconditional love and acceptance rather than performing for it. You are His beloved and He delights in giving you His kingdom! This invitation is not just for the spiritually elite or super-Christians. It's an invitation to all who are hungry and thirsty for true life found in Christ. Living from this reality produces outrageous and extreme joy. You are loved and pursued. Go ahead and believe it and declare it with confidence!

> *"I pray that out of the glorious richness of His resources He will enable you to know the strength of the Spirit's inner reinforcement – that Christ may actually live in your hearts by your faith" (Ephesians 3:16–17, Phillips Translation).*

QUESTIONS:

- The veil is torn and there is no gap between you and God. Are there any ways you are still living as if the veil remains a reality?
- What does it mean for you to live your everyday life from the reality that God is the One pursuing you?

DECLARATIONS:

- I am loved and accepted by God. He is pursuing my heart!
- There is no separation between God and me. I have full access to His presence!
- Christ is my inheritance. I will daily feast on His goodness!

ACTIVATIONS:

- Take a journal or a pad of paper and a pen with you to a quiet place. Ask God how He communicates His love to you. Spend some time listening and write down what you hear, sense, or think. Remember, He wants to communicate His love to you as a really good Father. Our heavenly Father speaks truth to us in a way that brings us into greater levels of freedom. The devil speaks in a way that makes us feel bad about ourselves. Make sure you are listening to the right voice.
- Take some time to rest in the New Covenant. You are in Christ and Christ is in you. Allow Him to fill your heart and mind with joy and peace in this reality. Go ahead and take advantage of your access and drink your fill of God's love!
- Think of practical ways to give God's love away to others throughout your day. How can you express His love today? Continue to do this every day. Receive freely and then freely give. This is how the kingdom of God flows.

CHAPTER FOUR

Freedom From Performance

few years ago, I was with a group of radical lovers of God, spending time with Him. We were all laying on the floor, soaking in God's presence. While I was lying there, I saw an inner vision in which I was working hard on a treadmill. As I was going for it on the treadmill, I heard the Lord speak. It was deep and profound! I heard him say, "Get off of the treadmill, son!" I understood partially what He was talking about in the moment, and gained further understanding as time went on. It was time to stop striving in my effort to see the things of God I desired to see. Not only was He talking about me performing to get His approval, which is the law in a nutshell, but He was primarily talking about striving and performing to see breakthrough in miracles. I was longing to see the power of God put on display so the world would know He is alive and active today. This is a passion of mine. But I thought I had to work hard to obtain more faith to see the miraculous.

As time went on, I realized I didn't need more faith; I already believed and had faith that God could and would demonstrate His power to heal and do miracles. What I needed was mind renewal. I needed to think differently about who God is, who I am in Christ, and the purpose for demonstrated power. From this encounter, I grew in the revelation that Jesus already paid for healing and miracles. It became much easier to partner with the Holy Spirit in seeing power flow through love. It became fun and enjoyable! It was simple for me ... "Get off of the treadmill, son!" In essence, God told me to stop striving in my own ability and learn to rest in what His Son has already accomplished.

Transformation and empowerment from heaven are found in this place of rest. It is amazing to me that Jacob received one of the most dramatic revelations from God while he was asleep (Genesis 28:10-17). It was in a place of rest that Jacob understood how heaven and earth were connected over his life. This open heaven reality over his life was according to God's promise and had nothing to do with Jacob's good behavior or hard work. We know this because, up to this point, Jacob was deceiving and not much of a role model. He laid his head on a rock when he had this dream. The rock symbolizes Christ. When we rest our head upon Christ and His finished works on the cross, we find ourselves mysteriously living in an open heaven reality without doing a thing to earn it! We will see much more ease in miracles when we learn to live from the abundance of His breakthrough.

TWO TREES

"For God knows that when you eat of it your eyes will be opened, and you will be like God, knowing good and evil" (Genesis 3:5).

There were two trees in the Garden of Eden. God actually empowered Adam and Eve to make choices. The fact that He did not remove their ability to choose wrongly reveals a lot about what He is like. He is not the micro-managing control freak who is deathly afraid of our wrong choices many of us portray Him as. It is important to know that God will always equip us to make choices that produce life. Life flows out of honoring and protecting relationship. The tree of life represents living from the inward compass of oneness with God. The tree of life is Christ Himself. We were meant to live in Him— the source of all life. The tree of the knowledge of good and evil represents the law, or living life by the rules based on performance. The deceiver knew the ramifications of humanity turning away from being governed inwardly from the heart and in relationship, to being governed externally by rules and punishment. He knew it would hinder the flow of heaven's government from being extended in the earth. The government of God flows out of relationship. It is important to understand that Adam and Eve chose the law when they chose the tree of the knowledge of good and evil. They chose a life of knowing right from wrong without the need for heart connection with their Creator. This is the law in a nutshell. The law was never God's choice, but He used it for our protection and as our schoolmaster until Christ came. It was for our protection because He had to judge sin before the cross. This was the ministry of all of the Old Covenant prophets—to judge sin. God introduced the sacrifices and rituals of the temple because He is just. Without the law, the sacrifices, and the prophets of old, all of humanity would have been toast! Thank God for His mercy. Now let's take a closer look at the lies the enemy used to lead Adam and Eve to feast on the wrong tree.

THE ULTIMATE LIE

Most of us have a grasp on the fact that the devil convinced Adam and Eve to disobey God's instructions and to make choices independent of Him. They chose not to protect their heart connection with God and their own disobedience had consequences. One major detail we can miss is that Adam and Eve were motivated to disobey the second they believed a lie.

The lie they were duped into believing was the need to do something to "be like God." What is so astounding is the reality that they were already like God! They were both created in God's image and likeness (Genesis 1:27). This means they were already like Him in nature. When God breathed into Adam, it did more than just bring him to life physically. God breathed the very life and nature (righteousness) of His Spirit into Adam. Adam became a living being in his spirit, soul, and body. The very breath of heaven brought Adam to life, and the first thing he saw was the face of God. Amazing!

The deceiver quickly convinced them to believe the lie that they had to perform to get what they already had. It was an issue of belief way before it became an issue of the act of disobedience. This is important for us to understand—most warfare is in the battle of our mind. It is a battle of what voice we are listening to and what we are choosing to believe!

The truth is Adam and Eve were already like God, and they were growing in the revelation of who He is and what He is like through relationship. This is the same for those of us who are in Christ. How many times are we duped into believing the same lie Adam and Eve believed? That we need to do something more or perform better to get what Christ already paid for in hopes that we will "be like God"? This is the weakness of the law given to Moses and the weakness of human effort to obtain the things of God. Don't get me wrong, the law was from God and it served a purpose. But God Himself made it very clear (even before the law existed) that the solution He was going to provide for the condition of fallen mankind was something entirely different than rules and regulations. "… he shall bruise your head, and you shall bruise his heel" (Genesis 3:15). This is a promise from God that He would send a Savior born of a woman, who would gain authority back and rule over the devil. From a biblical standpoint, the "head" symbolizes authority. The One God would send to do this of course is His only Son, Jesus the triumphant One! The devil certainly bruised the body of Jesus at the cross, but death could not hold Him down. He triumphed over death and completely stripped Satan of his authority at the cross. He took back the authority Adam and Eve lost, and now rules all of heaven and earth.

Notice the law given to Moses is not the cure for the sinful condition of mankind—Christ is! "For the law was given through Moses; grace and truth came through Jesus Christ" (John 1:17). The law was written and given to us on stones. Grace came to us in a Person! Jesus Christ was never meant to be reduced down to a doctrine or simply a message. He comes to us in person with the power to set us free and to keep us free!

WHY THE LAW?

The law was put into effect only because of sin. The law was meant to point out the fact that we are all lawbreakers and fall short of God's holy and perfect standards. It made the problem obvious so that God could lead us to the solution. The whole human race was under the bondage and condemnation of the law until Christ came. He alone has become the answer (read Galatians 3:19–29).

The works of the law cannot produce the righteousness of God because the law is powerless to change our inward condition. It can only point out the fact that we are sinners and have fallen short of God's holy standard. It's just like a police officer who can only point out to us when we break the law. They can deal with our behavior, but they are unable to change our heart attitude toward honoring the law, even though civil laws are for our own good and to protect us. They can only wait until we break the law again in order to point out the fact that we are a lawbreaker and then force the consequences.

The law of Moses demands perfect behavior but it cannot provide the means to change inwardly. We ought to be thankful for the law because without it, there would be no acknowledgement of sin and no need for Christ. Now that Christ has come and our faith is in Him, we have no more need for the law. According to Romans 7:1–4, we are now dead to the law and married to Christ "in order that we may bear fruit for God." Jesus alone came to restore the likeness and image of God in all who will put their trust in Him. It's only in Christ that we are empowered to "be like God." The works of the law and the efforts of man cannot change the human condition no matter how hard one tries. The law only has the ability to produce the fruit of guilt, shame, and condemnation. Why? Because it is based upon our ability to perform and all of us fall short of God's perfect standard. This is why grace is so amazing. Grace supplies and empowers us with the ability to live pleasing to God.

THE GRACE GOSPEL

Jesus, fully God and fully man, came and accomplished what no other human being has done or could possibly do. He perfectly obeyed the Father and fulfilled the righteous requirements of the law in our place. He accomplished what Adam and Eve failed to do. He obeyed His Father unto death and destroyed sin—the very thing that empowered the law and its ability to keep all of humanity imprisoned to its impossible demands (Colossians 2:13–15).

Because Christ has come, we no longer need to perform to get God's approval or try to be God-like in our own ability. Jesus alone accomplished this for us on the cross. Jesus fulfilled all of the law and the words given by the prophets, and administered a New Covenant. This means the Old Covenant is obsolete. We can learn from the old, but we no longer live by its standard of living. The New Covenant provides a higher standard of living through the Spirit. Godlikeness is restored to us simply by faith, and the fruit of this comes from learning to cooperate with the Holy Spirit. It is a work only the Holy Spirit can do on the inside of us as we remain yielded to Him. That's why the Bible calls it the "fruit of the Spirit." It's God-like fruit that is produced by a life filled with the Spirit and in rhythm with His heartbeat. We are no longer under the oppressive yoke of the Jewish law. We are under grace.

Grace is the undeserved favor of God freely extended to us in Christ. "For by grace you have been saved through faith" (Ephesians 2:8). Grace coming before faith tells us that we are presented with a free gift we did not work for or earn in any way. Even our faith does not make grace a reality. Faith is both the result and the response to the free gift in Christ. "So then faith comes by hearing, and hearing by the word of God" (Romans 10:17). The whole context of Romans chapter 10 is the gospel being preached. When the good news of the grace gospel is preached, faith springs up in the hearts of those listening. At that point, we are left with a choice to believe it and receive it with childlike faith or to continue on in our own human effort. God literally set the table for all of humanity! In Christ, we experience the benefits of having God's full approval and acceptance. Knowing Him is the greatest benefit. In this gospel of grace, we get Christ Himself and a brand new set of eyes to see through. Grace enables us to recognize the truth and empowers us to take action with faith.

> *"... that we might learn to praise that glorious generosity of His which He made us welcome (accepted) in the everlasting love He bears toward the Son. It is through the Son, at the cost of His own blood, that we are redeemed, freely forgiven through that full and generous grace which has overflowed into our lives and opened our eyes to the truth"* *(Ephesians 1:6–8 Phillips Translation).*

BY GRACE, THROUGH FAITH

"Even when we were dead (slain) by our own shortcomings and trespasses, He made us alive together in fellowship and in union with Christ; [He gave us the very life of Christ Himself, the same new life with which He quickened Him, for] it is by grace (His favor and mercy which you do not deserve) that you are saved (delivered from judgment and made partakers of Christ's salvation). And He raised us up together with Him and made us sit down together [giving us joint seating with Him] in the heavenly sphere [by virtue of our being] in Christ Jesus (the Messiah, the Anointed One). He did this that He might clearly demonstrate through the ages to come the immeasurable (limitless, surpassing) riches of His free grace (His unmerited favor) in [His] kindness and goodness of heart toward us in Christ Jesus. For it is by free grace (God's unmerited favor) that you are saved (delivered from judgment and made partakers of Christ's salvation) through [your] faith. And this [salvation] is not of yourselves [of your own doing, it came not through your own striving], but it is the gift of God; Not because of works [not the fulfillment of the law's demands], lest any man should boast [It is not the result of what anyone can possibly do, so no one can pride himself in it or take glory to himself]" (Ephesians 2:5–9 Amplified).

This passage of scripture in the Amplified translation is so rich and full of mind-renewing truth. Just the simple truth that God lifted us from being dead in sin and raised us up to give us joint seating with Christ is absolutely amazing. He did this to clearly demonstrate the riches of His free grace and kindness toward us. Wow! God could have simply stopped at saving us out of hell and promised us eternal life in heaven, and that would have been enough for us to give thanks for all eternity. But He didn't stop there! He restored our nature to its original design and restored our purpose to rule and reign with Christ. He did this all by grace. What a glorious salvation we get to partake of.

Notice how Paul says in the above passage that our salvation is by grace and through faith. As I have already stated, grace comes before faith. Grace is the free gift presented to us without having to work for it or earn it in any way. This free gift is our birthright. We have a right to what was paid for on the cross simply because we are children of God who are born of the Spirit. This is based on what God Himself accomplished on our behalf through his Son.

Faith, on the other hand, is our response to what He accomplished, and we simply need to believe in order to freely receive or access what was paid for. Everything Jesus paid for is already in our account without working for it. This is grace. It is our responsibility to believe the truth of what's in our account and then go and access what belongs to us. This is faith. Personally, I will speak out or declare with my mouth what I am accessing or partaking of, and then I will give thanks. The expressions of faith, according to Scripture, are speaking out of your mouth what you believe and then acting upon it. The action part of faith is the evidence that we truly trust God to be who He says He is and to do what He says He will do. Take healing, for example. Jesus already paid for the healing of the whole world. This is in my account based on the blood of Jesus. It is my responsibility to believe this truth and declare it to be true. The next step is to take action and begin to release healing to people around me. This is how I know I have faith for healing. A mustard seed size of faith is the only requirement to see mountains move. Mustard seeds are the tiniest seeds. That's encouraging to me! The other good news is our feelings don't need to match up with what we believe. The mature in Christ exercise their faith whether they feel it or not. The more we declare and act upon what we believe, the more our feelings will catch up with what we believe.

> *"Now faith is the assurance of things hoped for, the conviction of things not seen"* (Hebrews 11:1).

The grace of God is what produces the assurance and conviction of things hoped for and not seen. Grace produces faith. The more you and I experience the goodness and kindness of God, the more our faith will grow in taking Him at His word and acting upon it. This is the place where trust grows. This is the place where we get to know God as a really good Father.

OVERWHELMED WITH JOY

I was in San Francisco on a one-week outreach trip with YWAM in an intense part of the city. We learned about evangelism in the mornings and then went out to serve people and pray for them in the evenings. One afternoon I was hanging out with a few of the guys on the team, and I was really struggling with believing lies about myself. I was battling sin and really feeling like a failure because I wasn't walking in victory and freedom like I wanted to.

The guys started to pray, and I isolated myself from them because I was so angry with myself and dealing with shame. In my isolation, the Lord asked me a question: "What are you doing over here?" The Lord's question seemed to get right to the heart. I was behaving like a disgruntled orphan, so I didn't want to talk to the Lord in that moment. Then I heard Him say, "Go back over there and have them pray for you." After wrestling with what God had said, I finally went back over to my friends and asked them to pray for me. I was still rather grumpy and disgruntled and didn't think I deserved anything good from the Lord because in my mind I was a failure. As they were praying for me, something completely new and unusual happened. I got hit with what felt like a wave of goodness and joy crashing over me. I fell back on the floor and laughed hysterically for about 3–5 minutes. When the laughter subsided, I was completely refreshed and renewed both mentally and emotionally. The lies and sense of being a failure were just washed away. I realized that day that God truly is good, and His presence is freeing. I realized that I get what I don't deserve, and His grace changes everything. What I didn't know at the time was this encounter was meant to be an invitation to renew my mind and to know Him better. I still viewed this as just a special one-time event because I thought it was based purely on my emotional condition. I thought God just felt sorry for me. As time went on, I stepped into the revelation of sonship. I began to understand that He is the One pursuing me and I can experience His limitless and empowering presence on a continual basis.

The truth is God pours out on our lives because of the cross—because He is good. It's not because of how messed up our lives are. Grace is rooted in His goodness. Period. Sometimes I think we have a theology in the church that says God will only draw near to us if we come to Him desperate and broken. We attempt to twist His arm to show up by proving to Him how messed up we are. Somehow we think we deserve something from Him only if He feels sorry for us. If parents treated their kids like this, they would be labeled a dysfunctional family! Could you imagine a parent only showing affection to their kids if they are struggling with something? This is the lie I believed about God for many years. He absolutely loves us unconditionally, whether we are doing well or struggling. He is always present with us because of the sacrifice of His Son and because He loves us. We desperately need a theology rooted in the goodness of God back in the church. We have been reconciled and made one with God by His doing. We have the privilege of enjoying fellowship with Him 24/7 for the rest of our lives.

LIVING IN THE DIVINE INFLUENCE

Not only are we completely saved by grace, but we now live by grace. Grace is "the divine influence upon the heart and its reflection in the life, including gratitude" (Strong's concordance). Grace is the operational power of God which enables me to live Christlike in this world. This is what it means when Paul says: "And now the essence of this new life is no longer mine, for Christ lives His life through me! My real life is Christ—we live in union as one!" (Galatians 2:20 TPT). We no longer live in dependence upon ourselves to obey the commands of God; we are completely dependent upon the life of Christ working in and through us. This mystery is so great because His Spirit is joined to ours, and yet He doesn't remove our unique personalities as His life flows through us. Each one of us is a unique revelation of Christ Himself. As Paul says, "But we have this treasure in jars of clay, to show that the surpassing power belongs to God and not to us" (2 Corinthians 4:7). God does not remove our humanity from the equation. This is a beautiful mystery!

God gives grace to the humble. The humble are not those who think they have obtained personal virtue by their own disciplines and efforts. The humble are those who are forever wrecked by the revelation of Jesus and have come to know their absolute need for Him in all things. With this foundation in place, let's take a look at three aspects of the nature of grace found in the Greek language that continually pour into our lives. (The following definitions are from the BLB Lexicon.)

1. "That which affords joy, pleasure, delight, sweetness, charm, loveliness, favor ..." The top priority of grace is to enjoy the pleasures and pure joy of our union and intimacy with Christ. This is what we were created for. We were grafted into Jesus and became one spirit with Him. We increase in favor as we learn to live from the reality of abiding and remaining in the pleasures of our union with Christ. As dearly loved children, we are free to enjoy Him and to passionately pursue Him. I have noticed that in some circles, you can be quickly criticized as being religious or "works" oriented if you mention "seeking" God or "pursuing" the heart of Jesus. Some will say, "We are in union with Christ and already have all of Him. Why would we need to pursue Him?" The truth is I am in union with my wife, yet I will continue to pursue her heart in relationship for the rest of my life. True passion leads to the pursuit! I am complete and satisfied in my union with Christ, and at the same time I desire to know His heart more and more. I am hungry for greater measures of His Spirit to be poured out upon my life, my family, and my city. We cannot possibly contain all of God "for He gives the Spirit without measure" (John 3:34). He is side by side with me, and we are one in spirit. At the same time, He is above all and completely worthy of my adoration, worship, and wholehearted pursuit. Both our satisfying union with God and our pursuit of His heart is meant to be enjoyable. He is the focal point and the source of pure joy for all of humanity.

2. "Keeps, strengthens and increases us in Christian faith and Knowledge; the spiritual condition of one governed by the power of divine grace." Grace continually strengthens and increases us in our Christian faith and supplies us with everything we need to live in victory in every area of our lives. We are kept and sustained in victory by grace. Contrary to popular belief among some, grace is not a license to be irresponsible and live selfishly. Grace does not make allowance for sin to remain in my life. Living in sin is no longer our identity. The power of sin has been broken and we now have supernatural power to live our lives as Jesus did. Consider Graham Cooke's definition of grace: "Grace is the empowering presence of God that enables you to become the person that He sees when He looks at you." Grace empowers us to live a life of righteousness and holiness (Titus 2:11–13). This is our new identity! Grace lifted us out of our fallen condition, and grace also empowers us to live Christlike and victorious over sin and darkness.

3. "… affection, and kindles them to the exercise of the Christian virtues." Grace not only saves us and empowers us in righteousness, but grace also empowers us into our purpose in Christ. Grace is the empowerment upon our lives to take action with the gospel of power. The empowerment of heaven is at work in us to be who God says we are and upon us to show the world what He is like. I love how this definition of grace starts with the word "affection." God is love. If we are going to show the world what God is like with power, it must be demonstrated in love.

This is the limitless grace available to the humble—grace we were designed to live in continually. The law of Moses and grace cannot be mixed simply because we cannot perfectly obey the whole of the law in our own ability. The law requires perfect obedience. Therefore it is only by grace that we are saved and also empowered to live as Christ lived His life—in complete dependence upon Papa God.

QUESTIONS:

- What does it mean for you personally to be "dead to the law" and now married to Christ according to Romans 7:4? Are there areas of your life He is calling you to "get off of the treadmill" so you can enjoy the benefits of living by grace?
- Can you relate to the thinking that God only draws near when we have issues in our lives? How have you experienced God pursuing you just because He's good and He loves you?
- What has your experience and understanding been of how the law demands but grace empowers? How have your thoughts about grace changed after reading this chapter?

DECLARATIONS:

- I am dead to the demands of the law and alive in grace!
- I bear fruit to God because I am married to Christ. I am one with Him!
- All that Christ paid for is in my account. I access what's in my account through faith!
- I live in the pleasures and empowerment of abundant grace. God likes me!

ACTIVATIONS:

- Grace is a Person. Take some time to simply enjoy Him and allow Him the time to enjoy you. With childlike faith, receive the pleasures and the empowerment of His divine influence upon every part of your life. Welcome Him into specific areas of your life where you need victory or breakthrough. Grace is your new home!
- Meditate (fill your mind) on the benefits of living by grace and what that looks like in your daily life. Write down 3–5 specific things that you can see being transformed in your life or your thinking by grace.
- Declare this every morning: I am living from God's pleasure and acceptance. It is going to be a great day because God is for me!

CHAPTER FIVE

The Free Gift of Righteousness

"But now the righteousness of God has been manifested apart from the law, although the law and the Prophets bear witness to it – the righteousness of God through faith in Jesus Christ for all who believe. For there is no distinction: for all have sinned and fall short of the glory of God, and are justified by his grace as a gift, through the redemption that is in Christ Jesus ..." *(Romans 3:21–24).*

Being justified, according to the BLB Lexicon, means "to render, declare, pronounce or exhibit one to be righteous, or such as he ought to be."

You have been rendered and declared righteous by the Judge of all the heavens and the earth! He holds the highest place of authority to declare such a thing. This of course is by faith and apart from the works of the law. In other words, you didn't do a thing to earn this righteousness or to make it happen. The split second you believed what Christ accomplished in your place, you were completely 100% forgiven of all your sins and offenses that deserved punishment. Not only that, but you were instantaneously rendered, or declared righteous. It is a done deal in God's mind—as it should be in ours who believe the truth. Jesus came full of grace and truth (John 1:14). Grace transforms us into a new creation, and the truth transforms us to think like God. Truth renews our minds so we can see ourselves through the right lenses. Jesus is the embodiment of grace and truth, and He freely lives inside of you and me. This is the greatest scandal in history. We won the jackpot and didn't do a thing to deserve it!

The meaning of justified also tells us God "renders us righteous, or such as we ought to be." What does this mean? It literally means God restored us back to our original design in His image and likeness—as He created us to be.

Through the nature and effect of sin, the likeness of God was completely distorted on the inside of us. The part of our being that was like Him, and desired to be one with Him in nature and purpose, was enslaved to the task-master of what Paul describes as the "flesh" or the "sinful nature" abiding in us. Through Christ, the sin nature has been removed from our lives, and the righteousness and likeness of God has been restored on the inside of us. In Christ, we are "as we ought to be" in God's eyes.

This is not speaking of behavior modification or the ability to be a better person by doing righteous things. God re-created our nature in His own righteousness so that we can now manifest what He is like in the way we live. God literally changed our spiritual DNA. We are of the bloodline of Jesus now. In Christ, we are a completely new person! We simply need to believe what He did on the cross is enough.

God also puts us on exhibit and presents us as righteous. It's as if God is putting us on display and saying to the world, "Look at what I have done through My grace and kindness."

> "For we are His workmanship, created in Christ Jesus ..." (Ephesians 2:10).

We are His workmanship—His artwork of grace put on display for the praise of His glory! When we begin to believe what God has accomplished in us already through Christ, we will begin to also "exhibit" the righteousness and nature of God in our actions. Paul says in Romans 6:18 that we are now "slaves of righteousness" because we have been set free from sin. In other words, we are now prone to righteousness because grace empowers us in our new nature. Wow! Christ Himself is our righteousness and sanctification (1 Corinthians 1:30–31). It's not something we produce in and of ourselves. We are set apart in Christ, not by keeping the rules of the Ten Commandments or by our own effort. We only have Christ to boast in concerning the transformation of our inner world.

A WAKE UP CALL

One day, I was walking around evangelizing in the downtown area of my hometown in Washington State as I often did. My hometown is known for being heavily influenced by new age and the occult. I was very intense about sharing my faith, and at times I would find myself in arguments with people who thought differently than me. Sometimes I was gentle, but other times I would be very pushy in my approach. I would literally go up to people and call them to repent without sharing any good news. And I wondered why I didn't see many get saved outside of my family!

I remember having a sense of pride that day because, in my mind, I was proving my commitment to God with my works and by being bold. Boldly sharing my faith is where I found value and the confidence to know God was pleased with me. As I was walking around looking for targets, a scripture verse popped into my mind. I heard "Galatians 3:3."

I didn't exactly know what that verse said, so I decided to look it up and see what God was communicating to me. This is what I discovered: "Are you so foolish? Having begun by the Spirit, are you now being perfected by the flesh?" Wow! I instantly was cut to the heart, and I knew God was adjusting something in my thinking. It came in the form of a question, and the answer would reveal two things: The problem and the solution. It wasn't that God was telling me evangelism is bad. It was the thinking and motivation behind what I was doing that was bad. I was trying to perfect my commitment to God in my own effort and spiritual superiority. I was evangelizing for approval rather than evangelizing from approval! This truth was not revealed to condemn me, but rather to renew me and bring me into freedom. This set me on a long journey to understand that receiving grace was not meant to be a one-time event only at my salvation experience. I was created to live by grace and dependence upon the Holy Spirit in every aspect of my life. I am so thankful for times like this when my Father loves me enough to correct me. He disciplines the ones He loves, and it is always for our good (Hebrews 12: 5–7).

Now when I share my faith with people, my goal is to display the love and power of Christ to them rather than proving my devotion and commitment to God. I find great joy in sharing my faith with others from this heart position. True boldness comes from knowing you are loved rather than working for love. I am now seeing much more fruit in sharing Christ with others because I am living from acceptance and approval rather than for it. Love should always be what motivates us when sharing the gospel.

THE RIGHTEOUSNESS OF THE PHARISEES

"For I say to you that unless your righteousness surpasses that of the Scribes and Pharisees, you will not enter the kingdom of heaven" (Matthew 5:20).

What is the righteousness of the Scribes and the Pharisees? Simply put, it is self-righteousness. Somehow they thought they could attain to God's holy and perfect standard by their own effort and ability to keep the rules. The Pharisees actually added new rules that were burdensome and did not capture the heart of God, which is to love others. They looked for any opportunity to justify themselves and condemn others who fell short of their standards. When Christ came to save and to freely forgive, they were threatened by Him because it destroyed everything they built their lives upon. They were blinded to the grace of God because they would have to admit they too were sinners in need of forgiveness. They would have to admit their inability to be godlike based on their own righteousness. Embracing this reality would bring them down from their elevated place of pleasing man. This was not an option for them.

The only other righteousness that surpasses that of the Pharisees is the righteousness of God that comes by faith—faith in Christ's ability alone to restore godlikeness in us apart from the works of the law. One of the major errors I have heard in the body of Christ is the thinking that you should not preach too much grace because it gives people a license to sin. This line of thinking leads people to believe the remedy to this problem is mixing obedience to the Jewish law with grace. This thinking is absurd! This is the very reason why Paul used such harsh language with the Galatians. They were trying to mix the self-righteous works of the law with the free gift of grace. Listen to Paul's language to the Galatians:

> *"Oh foolish Galatians! Who has bewitched you? It was before your eyes that Jesus Christ was publicly portrayed as crucified. Let me ask you only this did you receive the Spirit by works of the law or by hearing with faith? Are you so foolish having begun by the Spirit, are you now being perfected by the flesh?"* (Galatians 3:1–3).

You would think Paul used such strong language for some hidden sin going on in the church. Hidden sin is a real issue to be dealt with and repented of, but this was not the case here with the Galatians. Paul was actually concerned for their salvation because they were being deceived to believe they could access the things of God by obeying the Jewish law, and yet still claim salvation in Christ. They wanted the best of both worlds!

Paul encouraged them to go wholeheartedly into the law or wholeheartedly into grace. Paul made it very clear they could not have both. The consequence of going wholeheartedly into the law is that it would cut them off from grace and salvation found in the Person of Jesus because the law demands perfection. Therefore, we cannot just pick and choose the parts of the law that we like or dislike. To obey the law is to obey the whole of the law. Jesus is the only Person who was able to accomplish this. This is why we cannot mix the two covenants. To attempt to obey the law cuts us off from the flow of grace. This same struggle is found in the body of Christ today, usually in working hard to get holiness and God's approval through lots of Christian activity. It's doing the right things for the wrong reasons, which I have already covered.

On the other side of the coin are those who preach grace in a way that judges others who do not hold to the same theology as they do. You may wonder, "How can one be stuck in self-righteousness when preaching grace?" Because we can use our theology as our standard, rather than having Jesus and His sacrifice to transform lives as our standard. We can easily take pride in our theology (even if it is a grace theology) and begin to criticize others who think differently. If what we believe does not lead us to genuinely love and honor others, I would question what our faith is in. We must preach pure grace, but we must remember that grace is a Person when doing so. The whole of the gospel is centered in God's Son. It is Christ who justifies us—not our correct theology. Some who preach a grace theology sometimes refuse to extend the grace they preach about to those who think differently than them. This doesn't sound much like Jesus. Right theology, yet missing the heart of God—much like the Pharisees!

THE CROSS—TRUE FREEDOM

Self-righteousness is such an ugly thing that can go undetected in our hearts. It is rooted in spiritual pride and self-reliance, and is always judging and criticizing others who don't seem to add up to our standards and beliefs. It is an attitude of the heart and an issue of an un-renewed mind. It is important to believe correctly, but it must lead us into a life of love. A great example of this is when the Pharisees and Scribes brought a woman caught in adultery to Jesus. The men who brought her were ready to kill her for her sins according to the law. Jesus brought them to the same playing field by saying, "Let him who is without sin among you be the first to throw a stone at her" (John 8:3–11). According to the law, everyone present had fallen short and needed what Jesus had to offer that day. The sad thing is, those men who were ready to stone her walked away and remained in their sin and self-righteousness. They lacked the humility it took to remain teachable and willing to receive from someone who thought differently than they did. In this case, it was the very Son of God who had the remedy to their separation from God's heart. Ouch!

Jesus will never condemn us in our sin. If we will just come to Him with an open and honest heart, He will always forgive us and free us from what imprisons our soul. Self-righteousness is any standard we use other than the cross of Christ. The cross is the only solution for sin and the transformed life. Our part is to repent (change the way we think) by agreeing with and believing the truth. It is the Spirit who changes us from the inside out. Love is always the fruit of the grace-filled and transformed life.

> *"For if, because of one man's trespass, death reigned through that one man, much more will those who receive the abundance of grace and the free gift of righteousness reign in life through the one man Jesus Christ"* (Romans 5:17).

> Faith: *"The leaning of your entire human personality on Him in absolute trust and confidence in His power, wisdom and goodness"* (1 Timothy 1:19 Amplified).

SEEING THE BLOOMING FLOWER

Quite a few years ago, I was praying about a specific person I was in ministry with. I will be honest … I was very agitated by this person's behavior and I was bringing to the Lord what "I was discerning in her." I was convinced she was the one who needed to change as I was bringing her issues to God in prayer. That didn't work out very well for me! As soon as the Lord had a chance to talk, He quickly changed my perspective. As I was praying, I saw a picture of a rose in my mind. The rose had thorns on the stem, but the flower itself was blooming. I heard the Lord say to me, "You only see the thorns, but I see the blooming flower!" Bam! Repentance hit my heart very quickly. I knew then that the one who needed to change was not her—it was me! All I could see were the rough areas of her life or the wrong thinking that she had. I wasn't extending much grace to her, and meanwhile God was working beautifully in her life. She had just recently surrendered her life to God again after coming out of a long season of rebellion. She still had some rough edges to her. She was in process as Jesus was restoring her life. Jesus was focused on the growth already happening in her—the progress currently happening. I learned through this experience that God celebrates progress, not perfection.

What was exposed in me was a critical and self-righteous attitude. I was measuring the spirituality of others based on my works and theology rather than the cross. This encounter became an invitation to know the heart of God better and to look for the positive growth in others who are in the process of transformation just like me. We have the privilege of looking for the evidence of what God is doing in a person and celebrating it. We have the privilege of loving and honoring people the way God does.

CALLED TO FREEDOM

We truly are free sons and daughters of God through the death and resurrection of Christ. We no longer live under the curse resulting from the fall of Adam and Eve. In Christ, we are justified as if we never sinned in the eyes of God. Sin no longer has power over us. We are declared righteous as God originally designed us. Now that we have this freedom, what do we do with it? What is the fruit and result of this freedom? Paul answers this question for us very clearly.

> *"For you were called to freedom, brothers. Only do not use your freedom as an opportunity for the flesh, but through love serve one another" (Galatians 5:13).*

> *"Do nothing from selfish ambition or conceit, but in humility count others more significant than yourselves. Let each of you look not only to his own interests, but also to the interests of others" (Philippians 2:3–4).*

We have been empowered by grace to serve others in love. Whether we are serving our spouse, our children, someone in the family of God, or radically loving on someone who doesn't know Jesus yet, this is our call. To be filled with the Spirit is to be filled with the love of God that leads us into action. Love always looks like something. It is more than a feeling—love is a verb! If we are truly surrendered to Christ and what He alone accomplished through His death and resurrection, then serving others through love will be evident.

The good news is when we truly yield to Mr. Grace Himself, loving others will be the natural outflow because it is in our nature to do so. We have power through the Spirit to choose love in any circumstance.

Notice Paul says to the Philippians that humility is counting others as more significant than ourselves. He doesn't say humility is demeaning ourselves. This is good news because many think putting ourselves down is the true mark of humility. This thinking is actually rooted in low self-esteem and can become very self-centered. It communicates to others, "Look how humble I am by tearing myself down!" This thinking is unwise. True humility looks for the greatness and significance of others, and true love looks out for the needs of others. Humility is not thinking less of myself, it's thinking more of others! If we were worth nothing, this wouldn't be significant. It really becomes significant when we realize the greatness God has placed in us, and then choose to value the greatness of others as more important.

Everyone expects a servant to serve, but no one expects a king to serve. This is the exact thing Jesus did as an example for us when He washed His disciples' feet. "Have this mind among yourselves, which is yours in Christ Jesus" (Philippians 2:5). What is this mind or way of thinking we should be having? The fact that Jesus was equal with God and understood He was a King and yet He humbled Himself as a servant to all. As the Father's beloved Son and soon to be ruler of the planet, Jesus chose to serve others in love. What a great King!

> "And from Jesus Christ, who is the faithful witness, and the first begotten of the dead, and the Prince of the kings of the earth. Unto Him that loved us, and washed us from our sins in His own blood, And has made us kings and priests unto our God and His Father; to Him be glory and dominion forever and ever. Amen" (Revelation 1:5–6).

God alone has made us royal kings and priests through the blood of His Son. It is with this understanding of our new identity and the greatness we have in Christ that we are called to serve others. Jesus never rebuked his disciples for desiring greatness. He simply redirected them to understand what greatness truly looks like in the kingdom of God (Mark 9:33–35). Royal sons and daughters confidently look for ways to be a servant to all. This attitude and approach to life diffuses the fragrance of Christ to the world around us.

QUESTIONS:

- How does it feel knowing God has declared you righteous and puts you on exhibit as a testimony of His grace? How have you been infused with the nature of God?
- Have you experienced people using a "grace theology" in an unloving and almost self-righteous way? How has your understanding of the nature and the fruit of grace changed?
- Have you ever thought of yourself as royalty? Do you believe God has designed you for greatness? Has low self-esteem hindered you in any way from living in this truth?

DECLARATIONS:

- I share in the righteousness of God as a free gift. I am a child of God!
- I diffuse the nature and the fragrance of Christ everywhere I go!
- I am empowered by grace to put the love of God on display!
- I am of the bloodline of Jesus. I am royalty. I am called to greatness!

ACTIVATIONS:

- Take some time to thank God for the free gift of His righteousness. Give radical thanks for His nature being infused in you in Christ.
- Ask God to help you see people through His eyes. Ask for the ability to see "the blooming flower." Intentionally celebrate progress and growth in others, and see how your attitude and perspective on life changes as a result.
- Take some time to meditate on the greatness you have in Christ. You are royalty! As a king and a priest in God's kingdom, look for ways every day to diffuse the fragrance of Christ through coming in low and serving. Where has God given you influence to serve?

CHAPTER SIX

Realities of Eden Restored

My hometown in Washington State is surrounded by beaches and the beauty of God's creation. As you can imagine, I loved going to the beach to spend time with God and to pray. One particular time, I went to one of my favorite beaches in the evening when the sun was setting. I decided to spend some time worshiping God on a huge rock. I was singing a simple children's song and telling the Father and the Son and the Holy Spirit how much I adored each one of them. When I got to the part of the song where I sang to the Holy Spirit, I was suddenly overwhelmed and very aware of His tangible presence upon me and all around me. Up to this point in my life with God, I had never experienced His manifest presence this strong. The only other time I remembered His presence like this was when I was baptized. I got baptized in the ice-cold bay in January, and when I came out of the water I was supernaturally warm all over my body with the presence of God. My mom touched my shoulder and was amazed at how warm I felt after being dunked in the freezing cold water. I was filled with so much gratitude!

This time on the rock was different, though. My encounter with God at my baptism came with tears and deep gratitude; this particular encounter on the beach came with extreme joy and a strong sense of feeling intoxicated. I don't know how else to describe what I was feeling. This experience with God was so much better and far more ecstatic in nature than anything I had ever experienced in the past. When I say ecstatic, I mean an intense joy and satisfaction beyond what words can describe—beyond anything the world offered me! My mind was so overwhelmed with the pleasure and peace of God. Someone truly would have thought I was drunk or out of my mind if they saw me stumbling on the beach that night. Honestly I didn't care what people thought at the time. I was literally stumbling around the beach as I was attempting to head back to my car. I was so overwhelmed by His goodness!

You need to know that I had no grid for what was happening to me. I was simply trusting that if I asked my Father for bread, He wouldn't give me a stone. King David says in Psalm 16:11, "… in Your presence there is fullness of joy; at Your right hand are pleasures forevermore." The word "fullness" here comes from the Hebrew word "soba" which means abundance, satisfying, or full.

The intense joy I was experiencing in His presence was so over-the-top abundant and satisfying. He is what my soul was always longing for!

THE PLACE OF PLEASURE

As I was walking back to my vehicle, I thought, "Father, can I feel this all the time?!" I was undone and I didn't want the feeling to go away. Somehow I thought I had to perform to maintain this level of joy and pleasure in His presence. This encounter led me to discover something that would change the rest of my life. I discovered the truth that I was created to have unbroken union with God through His Spirit abiding in me. I can enjoy Him any time and in any place. He has made His home in me, and I just needed to learn to make my home in Him. We were created to live in His presence on a continual basis. Christ came to restore this reality in our lives. He came to restore the realities of Eden back into our hearts.

Because the intense feeling I had in that experience faded over time, I believed the lie that I had to go from extreme encounter to extreme encounter to truly be satisfied. This belief led me into a lot of frustration. In our hunger and pursuit to know God more, we will have times of extreme encounters that are necessary for growth and acceleration into new territory. These encounters come out of our passion to know Him and to know His will. The truth is we can find continual joy and fulfillment in abiding in our oneness with Christ. Nothing has the power to separate us from Him. We have been grafted into Him and He is pure pleasure! This pleasure we find in Him is the reason we were created. God created Adam and Eve and placed them in the Garden of Eden. The word "Eden" in the Hebrew means "the place of pleasure." What a revelation and insight this gives us into the intentions of God. He created you and me first for the pleasure and delight of knowing Him and being one with Him. Everything else flows out of this joy-filled relationship.

The good news is we don't need to strive to get into His presence or to have an encounter. We can cultivate intimacy with Him and drink deep of His love continually from the heart. This reality is always available because of the sacrifice of Christ. It comes from a place of rest. Papa God placed us in Christ. This is not something we are trying to accomplish over again every day. It is a present and continual reality whether we feel it or not. It's just true! Christ Himself is our life source and He is a continual fountain of pure bliss.

We can draw from this fountain at any time, in any place, or in any circumstance. He re-created us for this. He re-created our hearts to be a beautiful garden where He could commune with us continually. He delights in us.

THE PLEASURES OF ONENESS WITH GOD

We have been placed right into the center of the Trinity. Grafted into the Father and the Son through the Holy Spirit. This is the place of pure, undiluted bliss! The amazing thing is God created humankind to be like Him in His nature and likeness. He breathed the very life of His presence and nature into Adam, and Adam became a living being in his spirit, soul, and body. This is what takes place on the inside of someone when they become born again. God literally infuses His Spirit into our spirit and we become one with Him. This is the greatest joy we can possibly experience in this life. The word infused or infusing means: "to cause to be permeated with something (as a principle or quality) that alters usually for the better." It's like tea being placed in hot water. The tea is infused into the water until it completely permeates the water with its flavor. It is altered forever with the flavor and quality of the tea. This is what happens when the Spirit is infused into us. We become completely permeated with the flavor and quality of heaven. We have been altered for eternity.

We see this as the very heartbeat and purpose of the Garden of Eden. God would walk with Adam and Eve in the cool of the day so much that they knew His sound (Genesis 1:8). Amazing! Because God walked with Adam and Eve in the Garden, the reality of His presence was all they knew before sin entered the world. This shows us that God first created Adam and Eve for relationship—to know Him and be known by Him. This is God's top priority.

There was nothing separating Adam and Eve from the very presence and goodness of God. They were one with God in union and in intimacy. In the Garden, there was perfect safety and full provision. They had everything they needed. God did not withhold anything good from them! There was no sickness, disease, poverty, or sorrow. In fact, there was no separation between heaven and earth. Heaven and earth were aligned in the garden. God would come to walk with Adam and Eve in the cool of the day to spend time with them. Of course we know the story—Adam and Eve believed the lie that God was withholding something good from them and they were kicked out of Eden. All was lost!

This is the reason why the gospel is such good news. Jesus came to restore and to recover all that was lost as the Champion of our salvation. He died as you and me and removed sin—the very thing that brought separation. The very moment we put our trust in Christ, we freely received what He purchased with His blood. We were instantly restored by grace into unbroken union with our beautiful Creator. God literally raised us from the dead, breathed and infused His life into us through His Spirit, lifted us up to be seated with Jesus, and grafted us into Himself (Ephesians 2:1–7). It's not just that we have been made clean by the blood of Jesus to approach God's throne—we have been grafted into the Godhead (John 17:20–26). We are a part of the family and share in the inheritance.

We have been placed into the kingdom of light—the kingdom of God's dearly loved Son where there is no separation between heaven and earth. Being delivered from the kingdom of darkness and transferred into the kingdom of light is not a process. This is an instantaneous work of grace (Colossians 1:11–14). Because He lives in us, heaven and earth are intertwined and connected everywhere we place our feet. Our lives have become heaven's access to earth. He's just looking for people to agree with who He is and what He is doing.

ABIDING IN THE VINE

To abide simply means to remain, dwell, or to continue to be present. It doesn't take sweat to abide. It literally means we have made Christ our home, and we are remaining in that place just as He has made His home in us (John 15:1–10 MSG). It is a mindset, an attitude, and a posture of the heart. Abiding is not found in a physical place. It is found in our union and connection with Christ. It's already a present reality; we just need to tap into it. Many times I will just stop what I am doing and simply turn my affections toward Christ. I will "lean into Him" and instantly I am aware of His abiding presence, peace, and the pleasure of intimacy with Him. Sometimes He speaks about specific things and other times we just enjoy one another. Either way, He is amazing and beautiful!

I was visiting some friends a few years ago who are on staff at the International House of Prayer in Kansas City. I decided to visit the prayer room and sat back to lean into the heart of Jesus even though I was a little distracted and not feeling much. At one point I almost left because I was so distracted, but decided to stay a little while longer. I was at the tail end of a mundane and somewhat dry season of my life. I needed to encounter Jesus face to face. In fact, that was my prayer for this quick, four-day visit.

In that moment of feeling distracted in my mind, I ended up having one of the most dramatic encounters of my life. I had a vision of Jesus walking up to me and placing His hands firmly upon my shoulders. He then leaned forward, forehead to forehead, and just looked into my eyes. He didn't say a thing.

What I felt welling up on the inside of me in that moment is very difficult to describe. I was experiencing His love and gentleness and at the same time His strength and fierceness. He is the Lion and the Lamb. My revelation of Him increased that day. As you could imagine, I was more than a little undone in the presence of my King! This encounter altered some major things in my life and set me on a new course with fresh passion and focus.

I later found out that this very act is a traditional Maori greeting in New Zealand called the hongi. Two men will join forehead to forehead, nose to nose, and eyes to eyes. The traditional understanding of the hongi is an exchange of the breath of life or the sharing of both men's souls. Through this exchange, the one being greeted is no longer considered a visitor. They are considered a person of the land who now makes this new land their home and shares in the duties and responsibilities of the native people. It is like a covenant. I understood this encounter much better after I learned about the hongi. He has made covenant with us through His blood and has shared the breath of His life and Spirit with us. We have been brought into His land and into His way of life. He is our home. We now share in the responsibilities and duties of His kingdom. We are not just visiting this land or experiencing this reality once in awhile. This is where we live!

THE RIVER FROM THE LAND OF PLEASURE

"Now a river went out of Eden to water the garden, and from there it parted and became four riverheads" (Genesis 2:10).

The Father provided Adam and Eve with a river that came out of Eden (the land of pleasure) to water the garden. The garden is where Adam and Eve got to know God's voice and to make their home intimately in His abiding presence. This is also where they received instruction from the Lord to learn the importance of obedience.

God had not sent rain to the earth yet, so this river from Eden was a continual flowing river that constantly watered the garden. Adam and Eve were completely dependent upon this constant river in order to live. Without it, nothing would survive or be able to reproduce. There was nothing Adam and Eve did to work for or earn the river flowing into the garden. It was a gift for them and God was its source. To me, this is a beautiful picture of the God-filled heart of the born-again believer in Jesus. What God did in the physical is now an inward reality for those who are redeemed. This is New Covenant reality. The garden of Eden is now found in our new creation hearts. Our hearts were created for Divine romance and constant interaction with the One who formed and fashioned us for Himself.

I want to propose that this river from Eden is a perfect illustration of the Holy Spirit Himself continually flowing into our hearts. We were designed to be continually filled with God. He fills us with Himself so we can enjoy relationship with Him first. He also fills us continuously so the life of His Spirit can flow out of us into the world around us. God is currently pouring out His Spirit on a continual basis and there is nothing we did to make this happen. This outpouring is due to the sacrifice of His Son on the cross alone. Every other river or stream flows from this one source of life, pleasure, and true fulfillment. He is the source, and we are completely dependent upon Him. We cannot truly live or bear good fruit without this river of life flowing into us. This is what Jesus describes in John 15 when He talks about abiding. This is what we were created for. Many people say they are in "the prophetic stream" or "the prayer stream" or "the healing stream," etc. I say we are in the "God stream" and every other stream flows out of Him—the true source. Why limit how God can manifest Himself through your life? Are we not, as Paul says, "behaving like mere men" (1 Corinthians 3:1–6) when we boast of being of one ministry stream or another?

I am not saying God won't call us to focus on specific things He is doing in the body of Christ and to learn and be equipped in a specific gifting, anointing, or ministry expression. There is nothing wrong with healing, prayer, or prophetic movements. We certainly need each other in the body of Christ. These things will automatically flow out of our lives as we stay filled with the Spirit. The true source of it all is God Himself and we were created first and foremost for Him. I say let's live in the very reality Jesus Himself lived in—an open heaven where there is no lack of the Father's love, presence, provision, and power. As it was with Jesus, so it is with us! We share in His inheritance as true sons and daughters of God. What belongs to Him belongs to us. We are co-heirs with Christ. The greatest calling on our lives as followers of Jesus is to be so filled with God Himself that we cannot contain Him. This produces the abundant fruit of a heart thrilled and filled with the very life of God. This is how Jesus lived His life.

"... that you may be filled [through all your being] unto all the fullness of God [may have the richest measure of the divine presence, and become a body wholly filled and flooded with God Himself]! (Ephesians 3:19 Amplified).

FOUR RIVERHEADS

Let's take a look at the Hebrew meanings of all four of the rivers that parted from that one river in Eden so we can better understand the result of a heart filled with God.

- The meaning of Pishon is "increase."
- The meaning of Gihon is "bursting forth."
- The meaning of Hiddekel (or the Tigris) is "rapid."
- The meaning of Euphrates is "fruitfulness."

Let's put these four meanings together in a sentence: "Increase bursting forth rapidly with fruitfulness!"

This is what you were born for—to increase and burst forth rapidly with lasting fruitfulness. There is only one source that can produce this kind of fruitfulness to burst forth from within our hearts consistently and there is nothing we can do to earn it. Our part is simply to believe and to remain yielded.

> *"On the last day of the feast, the great day, Jesus stood up and cried out, 'If anyone thirsts, let him come to Me and drink. Whoever believes in Me, as the scripture has said, out of his heart will flow rivers of living water.' Now this He said about the Spirit, whom those who believed in Him were to receive, for as yet the Spirit had not been given, because Jesus was not yet glorified" (John 7:37–39).*

Jesus first gives an invitation for everyone who is thirsty for the truth to come to Him and drink freely. The result of this drink would be "rivers of living water" flowing out of his/her heart. It is clear in this passage of scripture that the drink Jesus is offering to the thirsty is the Spirit Himself. Once you drink of the Spirit, the Bible says, "Rivers of living water" will flow out from your heart. Notice it doesn't say a river (singular) will flow out, but rather "rivers" (plural). There is one river continually flowing into your heart, and this river is the Holy Spirit Himself. We were created to continually drink Him in so that our hearts are continually filled to overflowing. Could it be that these rivers (plural) flowing out of our God-filled hearts are "increase bursting forth rapidly with fruitfulness"? I say yes! We were re-created in Christ Jesus to be increasingly fruitful on a consistent basis. Not occasional fruitfulness but consistent fruitfulness in every season!

We are like trees planted by streams of living water (Psalms 1:3). We didn't plant ourselves there. He did. We were created for this life-giving river. This comes from abiding in the Person of Jesus as yielded lovers. Continually drinking God the Holy Spirit into our hearts to where we can't contain Him. The result is He comes spilling out and bursting forth in every aspect of our lives. The key is staying yielded to the Holy Spirit and partnering with Him in what He is saying and doing. We have the great privilege and honor of getting to know Him and learning how to stay in rhythm with Him every day.

KNOWN BY HIM

Simply following the rules and behavior modification never produce lasting fruit. It's not even produced by following good methods for practicing the gifts of the Spirit. Methods are helpful tools, but if we rely upon these methods to successfully operate in the gifts, we will be left spiritually bankrupt when we don't see the expected results. Fruit that lasts and glorifies God is the goal. This comes from living in the reality that we are now married to Christ and made one with Him. I am thankful for all of the training schools in the supernatural. These schools are catalytic in restoring Ephesians 4 to the church. "Equipping the saints for the work of ministry." I have personally led quite a few ministry schools. I highly value these training and equipping environments where people of all ages learn to do the stuff Jesus did. However, we need to be intentional about the foundations of intimacy with God and identity in Christ in these environments.

My concern is people are learning to do supernatural things and will actually get results without developing their own personal history with God. This can be very dangerous. Jesus said that people would prophesy, cast out demons, and do miracles in His name, but that He never knew them (Matthew 7:21–23). Jesus never said prophesying, casting out demons, or doing miracles was wrong. The problem Jesus was warning us about is people learning to do supernatural things without being known by the One who Redeemed them. He also called them "workers of lawlessness."

This means people will operate in power under their own authority and not under God's authority. This is the same dangerous trap Simon the sorcerer from Samaria fell into (Acts 8:9–24). He wanted the power of God for his own profit and fame and had no desire to know the source of that power. The goal is to know God and to be known by Him. It becomes natural to bear fruit that glorifies the Father when we are intentional about developing our heart connection with Him. Then, when we prophesy, cast out demons, and do miracles, it's because we have learned to be in step with His heartbeat for people. This is where the supernatural becomes an expression of God's love.

QUESTIONS:

- What encounters with God have shaped your thinking in the way that you relate to Him? How is the revelation of God in those encounters still affecting your life today?
- Have you ever thought of your heart as being like the garden of Eden? How does living from a place of unbroken union and oneness with God change the dynamics of your relationship with Him?
- How is the river of God increasingly bursting forth out of you with fruitfulness? What does it look like for you to practically set aside time to turn your affection to God and lean into your heart connection with Him?

DECLARATIONS:

- I am complete and satisfied in Christ. I am one with Him!
- I am designed to make my home in God's presence. My life is an open heaven everywhere I go!
- I live in the continual river of the Spirit. I am increasing and bursting forth rapidly with fruitfulness!

ACTIVATIONS:

- Take a few minutes to lie down on the floor and simply invite God to come and enjoy you (you can turn on some worship if it helps). Ask Him to wash over you with His pure river of life. Drink in His presence deeply until you begin to experience the pleasures of your union with God.
- Give thanks for what He pours out on you. You have access to Him anytime and anywhere!
- Ask God to specifically show you what it looks like for rivers of living water to flow out of you in your community. Begin to pray into what He shows you with joyful expectation of greater fruit and breakthrough from your life.

CHAPTER SEVEN

The Eternal River

"And He showed me a pure river of water of life, clear as crystal, proceeding from the throne of God and of the Lamb. In the middle of its street, and either side of the river, was the tree of life, which bore twelve fruits, each tree yielding its fruit every month. The leaves of the tree were for the healing of the nations" (Revelation 22:1–2).

This is a beautiful description of the river of life and healing that is currently flowing from heaven to the nations of the earth. Notice the source of this continual river: It comes first from the throne of God. The throne of God is the place where He rules and reigns from heaven to earth. As sons and daughters of God, we are called to live with a "heaven to earth" mindset. This mindset is rooted in grace because it originates with God and what He is doing from a perfect world toward our broken world. The reality of heaven always carries the solutions we need. We get to agree with God and join in on what He is doing from this posture and mindset. Life and healing continually flow from God's throne to the earth, not death and sickness. It is God's nature to bring life to what is dead and to heal and restore what is broken. This is who He is and He doesn't plan on changing!

Next this verse says, "and of the Lamb." It does not say from the Lamb but "of the Lamb." The difference here is that this river (the pure Spirit of God) is literally flowing out of the Person of Jesus Himself. He is not just pouring out His Spirit from a container when we pray hard enough. This river of life and healing is continually pouring out from Jesus Himself. Christ Himself is the source of this river! Another important thing that caught my attention in this passage is the fact that he describes Jesus as "the Lamb" here instead of King or Savior. This is specifically referring to Christ's sacrifice on the cross. When He was struck, water came gushing out of Him that would satisfy the longing of the human heart for all of eternity. Jesus Christ, the Lamb of God who was slain before the foundation of the world, is the fountainhead of this river of pure joy, life, and healing to the nations. His sacrifice was enough to fill every thirsty heart on this planet for all of time. We live from the abundance of Christ and His sacrifice, not from lack.

THE SPIRITUAL ROCK

"All ate the same spiritual food, and all drank the same spiritual drink. For they drank of that spiritual Rock that followed them, and that Rock was Christ. But with most of them [Israel] God was not well pleased, for their bodies were scattered in the wilderness" (1 Corinthians 10:3–5).

When Moses was commanded to strike the rock in the wilderness, water came gushing out to give drink to all of Israel. According to Paul, this rock was Christ. This rock actually followed Israel everywhere they went to give them continual drink so they would not die in the wilderness.

The first time Moses struck the rock, it symbolized Christ being punished according to the law for the sins of the whole world. Moses symbolizes the law, so it makes sense that God commanded him to strike the rock. Like the rock in the wilderness, when Jesus was struck, the heavens burst wide open and a river of life and healing came gushing out of Him. Spiritual drink was released for all who would come and receive freely from Him. Interestingly, God commanded Moses to speak to this same rock so that water would come forth a second time. Moses got angry with the children of Israel and struck the rock again instead of speaking to it. This was the very act that kept Moses out of the Promised Land. Have you ever wondered why God seemed so harsh by not letting him enter the Promised Land? It's because the law cannot inherit the promises of God no matter how hard it tries. It's only by grace, through faith, that we inherit the promises. The rock was Christ and He could only be struck once for the sins of the whole world. Once He was struck, there would be no more punishment for sin. This is why Moses was commanded to speak to the rock instead of striking it again. We are now required to approach Christ by faith and speak directly to Him. Faith is first expressed through speaking out what we believe. Speaking to the rock also points us to the sweetness of our union and intimacy with Christ.

> "Oh, that My people would listen to Me, that Israel would walk in My ways! ... He would have fed them also with the finest of wheat; and with honey from the rock I would have satisfied you" (Psalm 81:13–16).

Here are a couple of cool facts about honey: Honey is used as a 100% natural sweetener. It was also used in history as a natural cure to promote healing. Christ is the 100% sweetener to our bitter lives and healing to our brokenness. God's intent is to fully satisfy the whole world with continual water and honey from the Rock. Christ Himself is the satisfying drink of pure grace that all of humanity is longing for! Our lives are meant to be a testimony of this sweetness we find in Him.

SECRET PLACE OF ANOINTING

I was at the store one night, getting a few groceries for my wife. While I was there, I was putting a lot of pressure on myself to step out and demonstrate the power of God to someone. So many Christians live under this pressure to produce results for God, especially when it comes to evangelism. I lived under this heavy pressure for years, and it still tries to "eat my lunch" every once in a while. As I was walking through the store and feeling frustrated, I heard the Father say to me, "Just enjoy My presence." Something shifted in my focus. I relaxed and simply turned my focus upon Him and postured my heart to a place of connection. I instantly was aware of the goodness of His presence. I have learned that His presence does not come and go or ebb and flow. The Holy Spirit is upon us to remain just like He was with Jesus when He got baptized (Matthew 3:13–17). Sometimes we just need to "lean into" Him to be aware of His already abiding presence. He is so good!

Before I knew it, I had naturally approached two people in need of the love of Jesus and they both encountered God. I was free from pressure and it was fun to simply love on these two people with the love and power of God. One woman received healing in her tailbone and was amazed and so happy that God cared for her in that way. I gave her my phone number and she called me weeks later to tell me that she did not need a shot any more to relieve her of the extreme pain she was constantly in. She was completely pain free. Yay God! A broken world is waiting for us to learn how to enjoy God in all of life. This is where His love and presence flows. The place of His anointing flowing through our lives in increasing measures is found in the place of enjoying Him. I am not saying we enjoy Him to get something. It's just natural for the Anointing of His presence and power to flow out of a place of rest in His love. We are anointed with His presence and power whether we feel it or not. It's just true.

THE FIRST OUTPOURING

The first thing Jesus did after He was raised up to the right hand of the throne was to pour out His Spirit. His death and resurrection broke the floodgates wide open! This first outpouring was not a one-time event; it is a present and continual flow from heaven to earth simply because Jesus alone is the source. His faith opened up the heavens, not ours. Some teaching uses Acts 2 as a blueprint on how to access an outpouring or a revival. The idea is if we come together in unity, prayer, and repentance, then God will come down in revival and power. The problem with this is the disciples in the upper room did not do these things to get God to pour out His Spirit. Jesus instructed them to wait in Jerusalem for the promise of the Spirit. They were in unity and prayer as a response of faith to the promise. They were all believing and waiting for the same thing. It was the promise given that enabled them to come together and believe for it. There was no striving involved, just believing. God is not reserving outpourings of His Spirit for special times and on special occasions. He is not withholding the goods until we get our ducks in a row. He is the One pursuing all of humanity.

Some say revival won't come unless we repent first. Jesus said, "Repent, because the kingdom of heaven has come near" (Matthew 4:17 HCSB). He didn't say repent and then the kingdom of God will come. He instructs us to repent because the kingdom of God has already come near. When we perceive the presence of the King, then we will perceive His kingdom. Our repentance can't earn the promises of God! Our repentance serves to open our eyes to the reality of who God is and what He is already doing in our midst. The kingdom is both present and increasing in the earth. The kingdom increases every time we collectively agree with Him and His purposes. Many are living with the mindset of occasional outpourings rather than a continual outpouring of His presence. The flow of heaven wants to constantly pour into us and overflow out of us. We are the carriers of this river of life and He wants to burst out of us onto dry places everywhere we go. We bring life to death and hope to despair. The whole earth is parched and longing for the drink we carry inside of us. We are the carriers of revival!

NO DESERT SEASONS

In Christ, there are no desert seasons (Isaiah 35:1–10). The Spirit on the inside of us is a continual fountain of life and satisfaction. We do not live for fulfillment and satisfaction like the rest of the world. We live from a place of satisfaction in Christ. The key is to remain soft and yielded to the Lordship of Jesus. If we allow bitterness and self-seeking to take over, we shut off the valve to the water supply. The supply is still flowing from heaven, but we are not experiencing its delight and pleasure due to forgetting who we are in Christ. We were created for the pleasures of God and we are empowered with the responsibility of keeping a big YES in our hearts to Him.

Israel wandering around the mountain in the desert was never God's idea in the first place. They wandered around in the desert because of unbelief and disobedience. God was not pleased with them because of the hardness of their hearts. If we find ourselves stuck in a desert season, it may be due to hardness of heart or unbelief. We may be called into dry places to bring life to it, but we ourselves will never be dried up and isolated if we stay full of the Spirit. Just as important as staying full of the Spirit is staying connected to the body of Christ in healthy relationships. No one is designed to be isolated and on their own. We truly need each other. When we isolate ourselves from others we quickly dry up spiritually and become susceptible to lies and deception. Maintaining accountability and a teachable attitude sharpens us and propels us into greater levels of growth in the presence of God. There is power when we agree with each other in prayer and look for ways to bring encouragement to each other during hardships. There will be difficult and trying seasons in life for all of us. Most of us have faced circumstances of loss and trials that test our faith. Through these tests in life, we can rely upon one another and choose to stay anchored in the goodness of God. The greatest strength we can find in these times is in our union with Christ. Look at what Psalm 84:6–7 says. This is totally New Covenant reality!

> "Blessed are those whose strength is in you, in whose heart are the highways to Zion. As they go through the valley of Baca (weeping) they make it a place of springs; the early rain also covers it with pools. They go from strength to strength; each one appears before God in Zion."

No matter what the circumstances are, we can make it a place of springs and grow in strength because our hearts are set on pilgrimage. We were designed to pass through the valley of Baca (or weeping). We were not designed to live there. As we learn to make our difficult seasons a place of springs, we can help refresh others in their difficult seasons. Our lives will be like water to spiritually dry ground for those who are hurting and desperate for new life and purpose.

INTOXICATING LOVE

"Oh God, how extravagant is Your cherishing love! All mankind can find a hiding place under the shadow of Your wings. All may drink of the anointing from the abundance of Your house! All may drink their fill from the delightful springs of Eden. To know You is like enjoying a flowing fountain, drinking in Your life, springing up to satisfy. In the light of Your holiness, we receive the light of revelation. Lord, pour out Your unfailing love on those who are near You" (Psalm 36:7–10 TPT).

God wants to continually delight you with unhindered and unbroken love. Your heart was created to be filled to overflowing with God Himself. As the scripture above says, God's love is extravagant. His love is not just to be agreed with or stored away as one of our valued doctrines. His intoxicating love is to be drunk down and experienced deep in the heart. There is abundance in this place and you may drink your fill from the delightful springs of Eden at any time. Just simply turn your affection toward the Lover of your soul and receive freely with a thankful heart. When you drink in the very life of God, you will know what it means to be truly satisfied. Then you will thirst for more! This is something the world cannot offer the human soul. The world can offer you a counterfeit pleasure, but it will be short lived. Many times we are still enticed by the pleasures of this world because we don't know we can truly enjoy the pleasures of God. He created us to be the object of His outrageous love and delight! Being in union with Christ is pure bliss. Let's be enticed by His goodness, and not what the world offers.

QUESTIONS:

- How are you presently experiencing the eternal river of the Spirit? Would you say you are living with the mindset of occasional outpouring or continual outpouring? What do you believe is the outcome of each mindset?
- What are your thoughts on desert seasons after reading this chapter? How can you make your present circumstances a "place of springs"? How can you refresh and bring encouragement to others who are going through hard circumstances?
- Would you say your relationship with God is enjoyable?

DECLARATIONS:

- I live in the continual outpouring of heaven. I live according to promise!
- I bring the life of God into dry places. I carry revival everywhere I go!
- God's delight is in me. I am the target of His intoxicating love!

ACTIVATIONS:

- Imagine yourself under a continual waterfall of pure life and healing. Invite Jesus to speak to you in this place. What is He saying to you? What are you experiencing in the waterfall of His presence?
- Take some time to think about difficult seasons you have faced and how you made it a place of springs. Share with someone what you experienced and release that same encounter to them to bring refreshing and encouragement. The river of life longs to flow out of you!

CHAPTER EIGHT

New Creation Identity

I remember my thoughts very vividly as I drove to a revival service on a Friday night at Bethel Church in Redding, California. I was with my fellow students and leaders from my Discipleship Training School at YWAM in Chico, California. I had heard how God was moving at Bethel and I was very fearful that I was somehow going to be deceived by the devil in this service. I had my defenses up before even stepping foot into the building! As worship was going, I began to notice people around me physically being touched by the Holy Spirit. In my mind, it was not God! I was very concerned and even more convinced that my fears were the truth. People were very passionately seeking and worshiping God. This was definitely out of my comfort zone! I don't remember the message or even who spoke that night, but I do remember the invitation at the end of the service. It was a call to whoever was hungry for more of God to come up front. They had lines for people to stand in and wait for someone from the ministry team to come and pray for them.

I remember the tension going on inside of me, but I had made up my mind. I told the Lord that I was going to go up front, and this is what I said to Him: "If this is You, I want it. If this is not You, I don't want it!" I decided to take a risk and believe that God was big enough to keep me undeceived. As I was standing at the line waiting for prayer, a young man came up to me and gently laid his hand on my chest. I instantly experienced heat shooting through my chest and before I could think through what was happening to me, I fell back on the floor. As I was lying there on the floor, I heard the voice of my Father and He was saying one phrase to me over and over. He kept saying, "I love you, son! I love you, son! I love you, son!" I was completely wrecked by His love in that moment. His love chased away my fears and I felt so free. A weight lifted off of my shoulders and something dramatically changed inside of me. When I finally got up off the floor, I went around hugging people from my school and telling them I loved them. They were wondering, "What happened to Stephen?" It was dramatic and had lasting fruit in my life. I knew I would never be the same after this experience with the Father's love.

This was the beginning of a total life change from old to new in my thinking. As I experienced His generous love more and more, I began to believe deep in my spirit that I am a delighted-in son. This is the place where we stop thinking like orphans and begin to live from abundance in Christ as beloved sons and daughters. We no longer need to prove ourselves because we have made our home in His presence. Orphans are deficient of love. Beloved sons and daughters live with a sense of acceptance and abundance. The greatness of our destiny and purpose is directly connected to the truth of our new identity in Christ.

ALL THINGS MADE NEW

"Therefore, if anyone is in Christ, he is a new creation. The old has passed away; behold, the new has come" (2 Corinthians 5:17).

One of the most amazing things to me about God is how He can take someone broken and corrupted by sin and make them completely new. From the beginning of time when mankind first chose sin in the Garden, the human race has been working hard at "self-helps" and trying to fix our fallen condition. When this mindset creeps into the church, we find suffocating hearts masked by the performance of church attendance, being a good tithe payer, and following the rules to be a good person. What I just described is powerless Christianity 101! It's also known by the alias "religion" or "dead works." Unfortunately, this problem currently exists in many church communities. The good news is Father God offers all of humanity something entirely different and entirely better.

God is not a mechanic. When it comes to the fallen condition of His treasured creation, He does not fix or attempt to improve the old. He crucified our old corrupted nature inherited by Adam with Christ on the cross. He completely makes us a new creation altogether! He refuses to simply fix our old sinful nature, and He doesn't leave room for the old to mingle with the new. We are either in the new nature in Christ, or we are in the sinful nature inherited by Adam. We cannot be in both. We were born with the sin nature inherited from Adam, but the good news is we get instantly grafted into Christ through responding to the gospel. He alone is the solution! Found in this good news is the offer to be instantaneously delivered from darkness and brought into light. We were lifted by Grace Himself out of the pit of our fallen condition and seated with Christ in heavenly places. The intentions of God are not to make bad people good, but to raise spiritually dead people to life! It was nothing we did that caused God to want to redeem us. We don't deserve this new life in any way, shape, or form. This is completely a work of grace. God treasures us so much and He knew there was nothing we could do to get ourselves out of the mess we were in. We were spiritually dead, and He came to raise us from death into newness of life.

KAINOS

The word "new" in 2 Corinthians 5:17 above comes from the Greek word "kainos." The understanding of kainos is to be unused or unworn—literally "of a new kind," "unprecedented," or "unheard of" in substance and nature. It is something entirely unheard of or thought up by the mind of man. We are literally not of this world!

Our new creation identity is found only in the Person of Jesus Christ who invites us to be a partaker of His divine nature (2 Peter 1:3–4). This unprecedented and unheard of work of grace, which He has accomplished in us, is a present reality for those who are in Christ. The truth is, our minds need to be renewed to the truth of our new-creation identity. It is not an issue of our nature still needing to be changed because He already did that instantaneously at the cross—it is an issue of right believing! Jesus came full of grace and truth. Grace transforms us and empowers us in Christ. Truth transforms us by renewing our minds so we begin to think about ourselves like God does. It's time we see ourselves the way God sees us!

So what does it mean to be "in Christ?" Is it a figure of speech or is it a present reality to be experienced in this life? I choose to believe along with the Apostle Paul that "the old has passed away; (or died) behold, the new has come." It is already a done deal for the believer in Jesus. "Behold" refers to seeing. May the Spirit of God give us eyes to see what has already been accomplished through Christ, and help us to wrap up our identity and value system in Him alone! If we are "in Christ," then that means we are a new person all together. The old sinful nature in Adam is dead and gone. All of creation is groaning and longing for what we have become in Christ!

DEAD TO SIN AND ALIVE TO CHRIST

"… we have concluded this: that one has died for all, therefore all have died; and He died for all, that those who live might no longer live for themselves but for Him who for their sake died and was raised" (2 Corinthians 5:14–15).

When John the Baptist saw Jesus coming to the river Jordan to be baptized, he said something very profound which would change the whole course of history. "Behold, the Lamb of God, who takes away the sin of the world!" (John 1:29). Many throughout history have misunderstood this simple truth. Some say the blood of Jesus covers our sins. This is far from the truth! If our sins only need to be covered, then there was no need for Christ. The blood of animals used in the Holy of Holies in the Old Covenant temple had the ability to cover or appease God's wrath against sin. Jesus did much more than this. The priests of old were obligated to sprinkle the blood of animals over and over again to cover the sins of the Jewish people. They would still be prone to sin even after the blood of animals was sprinkled to find forgiveness. Why? The blood of animals never had the ability to remove the sin nature itself. Only Jesus had the ability to destroy the power and stain of sin once and for all time (Hebrews 7:27). He came to destroy the power of sin and to take it away for good—to remove the very thing that brought separation and death to all of humanity. He came to make right what had been corrupted and made wrong.

At the cross of Christ, we literally find a revolution in nature. It's a complete take over, if you will. Brace yourself because here is the bold truth: If you are in Christ, then your old sinful nature is dead. This is a great mystery and sometimes hard to understand. Somehow, mysteriously and by faith, we were included in Christ's death on Calvary. Jesus didn't just die for your sins; He literally became sin so that when He died, the power of the sin nature died with Him! God Himself destroyed the sin nature that was passed down from Adam. In exchange, we become the righteousness of God. Amazing!

In Christ, your sins are forgiven which means the offense is removed. Jesus took your punishment. He also took away your sin nature which caused you to be an enemy to God and prone to rebellion. He does not plan on giving your sin nature back to you! At your baptism, you were mysteriously united with Him in His death. You were co-crucified with Christ, which means you have been freed from the power of sin. Let's take a look at Romans 6 to gain a better understanding of this. (Please read all of Romans 6 before continuing.)

BAPTISM INTO HIS DEATH

"Do you not know that all of us who have been baptized into Christ Jesus were baptized into His death? We know that our old self (sinful nature) was crucified with Him in order that the body of sin might be brought to nothing, so that we would no longer be enslaved to sin. For the death He died He died to sin, once for all, but the life He lives He lives to God. So you also must consider (or reckon) yourselves dead to sin and alive to God in Christ Jesus. For sin will have no dominion over you, since you are not under law but under grace" (Romans 6:3, 6, 10–11, 14).

There is no mincing of words here with Paul. If you have been baptized into Christ, then you were (past tense) co-crucified with Him so that sin no longer has power over you. We are no longer slaves to a driving force inside of us, pushing us toward a destructive lifestyle as enemies of God. We are royal sons and daughters who may approach the very throne of our Father with boldness because of the blood of Jesus. We are of a new bloodline now. The key is to align our belief system to this whole new reality in Christ and reckon ourselves dead to sin and fully alive in God.

Interestingly, the word "sin" is used 16 times in Romans 6. It is used as a noun 15 times and as a verb only one time. This tells us that Jesus didn't just come to deal with our sinful behavior, but He came to conquer and defeat the taskmaster of sin residing in our hearts. It was as if sin had a personality and a will of its own. This is why the Jewish law or our own efforts at good behavior are not enough. Our efforts cannot possibly remove this driving force called sin from the very fabric of our soul and spirit. Jesus alone conquered and destroyed the nature of sin on the cross. It was a deathblow to the very thing Satan used to rule the hearts of mankind. When you were born again, the master of sin was removed and a new Master moved into your heart. Christ is now your new Master and He rules you with kindness and empowers you with grace and truth.

Grace frees us completely from sin and empowers us in righteousness. We now have access to the resurrection life and power of Jesus in all aspects of life. He didn't make us a good person or give us a moral code to live by. He raised us from the dead through the Spirit of holiness! He has made His home on the inside of us and He will not share His home with the old taskmaster. We were co-crucified, co-buried, co-resurrected, and lifted up to co-reign with Christ in heavenly places. You and I didn't do a thing to deserve this status. We just simply need to believe. This grace is outrageous!

WHAT ABOUT ROMANS SEVEN?

When I teach new creation, I always get asked about Romans 7. Many teach that Paul is describing his struggle with the sin nature still at work in him as a follower of Jesus. Many who take this stance will often say, "If you preach too much grace you will give people a license to sin!" I say if we believe and preach that we still have a sinful nature at work within us, then we will sin by faith. This mindset, in my opinion, is empowering a life of defeat and confusion. Grace empowers us to live out and manifest our new nature in Christ, not to stay in the struggle against sin! Let's take a closer look at what Paul is describing in Romans 7 in order to help us understand the context of it fitting with Romans 6.

> *"Or do you not know, brothers – for I am speaking to those who know the law – that the law is binding on a person only as long as he lives?" (Romans 7:1).*

To fully understand the bottom-line points a writer wants to get across, sometimes we need to know who the audience is. Who is the author writing to? In this case, Paul is clearly writing to believers in Rome "who know the law."

> *"Likewise, my brothers, you also have died to the law through the body of Christ, so that you may belong to another, to Him who has been raised from the dead, in order that we may bear fruit for God. For while we were living in the flesh, (past tense) our sinful passions, aroused by the law, were at work in our members to bear fruit for death. But now we are released from the law, having died to that which held us captive, (past tense) so that we serve in the new way of the Spirit and not in the old way of the written code (present tense)" (Romans 7:4–6).*

Paul is making it clear that those who were once living for God under the law were living by the flesh, and the law only served to arouse their sinful passions. Now that they belong to Christ, they are now living by the new way of the Spirit. This is a revolutionary change in thinking. The law only works to point out our sinful nature and holds us captive to sin's destructive ways. In Christ we are freed from the sin nature and empowered to bear fruit for God. Living by the flesh or sinful passions is something of the past for those who are now in Christ. Let's look at a couple more verses.

"The very commandment [law] that promised life proved to be death to me. For sin, [the task master–noun] seizing an opportunity through the commandment [law] deceived me and through it killed me. For we know that the law is spiritual, but I am of the flesh, sold under sin. For I do not understand my own action [living by the law]. For I do not do what I want, but I do the very thing I hate. Wretched man that I am! Who will deliver me from this body of death? Thanks be to God through Jesus Christ our Lord" (Romans 14–15, 24–25a).

It is very clear here that Paul is describing himself under the law and apart from Christ. He is describing the inner turmoil and struggle of a person who puts their mind to obeying the law but who is still held captive by the sinful nature. Paul gives the solution at the end of the chapter. Jesus Christ our Lord is the answer. This understanding lines up with Paul exhorting us to "reckon ourselves dead to sin and alive to Christ" and reminding us "sin shall no longer have dominion over you" in Romans chapter 6.

According to Paul, as he addresses believers in most of his letters, we are now saints and no longer identified as sinners. We are identified with Christ and what He alone has accomplished in us through the cross. We have been co-crucified and raised to life in Him. This truth is revolutionary and is the very gospel Paul preached. We now live in the resurrection life and freedom of Christ through the Spirit as Paul describes in Romans chapter 8.

"There is therefore now no condemnation for those who are in Christ Jesus. For the law of the Spirit of life has set you free in Christ Jesus from the law of sin and death" (Romans 8:1–2).

This is the conclusion to Romans 7. You cannot understand Romans 7 if you isolate it and do not read it in context, which includes the chapters before and after it. We have been freed completely from the law of sin and death by the Spirit of life. We either believe what Jesus did on the cross was enough or we don't. The Spirit of Christ lives in us, therefore the battle with the sin nature is over. This doesn't mean we won't ever be tempted to choose sin, it just means we have the power to say no.

A MIND-RENEWING ENCOUNTER

In 2010, I was a student at Bethel School of Supernatural Ministry in Redding, California. A very important part of the school for me was spending time in my Revival Group with other students who were also hungry for Jesus. (Revival Groups are groups of 65-70 students with a staff pastor.) One day our group decided to spend time soaking in God's presence and allowed Him time to love on us. As I was lying on the floor enjoying God's presence, I had an encounter where Jesus visited me in a vision. (This was an inner vision in my spirit.) I saw Him walk right up to me and He placed a robe around me, and put a ring on my finger and sandals on my feet.

He didn't say a word to me, but I felt His pleasure and delight in me as He was communicating through His eyes and His actions. This of course is right out of the prodigal son parable in Luke 15. This was a life-changing encounter for me. It was important for me to understand the significance of these three items He placed on me in order to be renewed in my thinking about my new identity.

- **The robe:** This symbolizes righteousness and favor (Isaiah 61:10). I am not just a hired hand to get the work done on my Father's farm. I am a chosen and favored son who has been completely restored to righteousness as He originally designed me. The filth has been removed from my sinful living. He didn't just cover my filth; He removed it and replaced it with His own nature. I am affectionately loved and valued by Him. I live in His smile and approval over me!

- **The ring:** This symbolizes sonship and authority. I have been given authority as a cherished son to proclaim and to demonstrate the kingdom of God everywhere I go. The spiritual world now knows who I belong to because of the ring on my finger. They know I have jurisdiction over darkness no matter where I am because Jesus has all authority in heaven and earth. I have been given authority to set captives free and release prisoners from their captivity to darkness. Slaves or servants do not carry this kingdom authority. Only loved and delighted-in sons and daughters do. This is who we are, and this truth is what produces confidence in us.

- **The sandals:** This symbolizes walking in the greatness of my new identity, purity, and purpose. I must add action to what I believe and live it out. I was created to destroy hell for a living and extend the borders of His kingdom through His love. Understanding how God sees me empowers me to live in my new identity with joy and confidence.

When you know the heart of the Father and what He is declaring over your life, you can face anything with grace and courage. This is what He wants for all of His children. We simply need to see ourselves as He sees us. The only possible way we can fulfill the great commission is if we come to know and believe the truth of who we are in Christ—the truth of who really lives on the inside of us!

If I believe I still have a sinful nature, then I will spend most of my time focused on trying to manage my issues rather than living in victory over them. We are living from the victory of the cross, not for it! Purpose and destiny always come out of identity.

WHY CHRISTIANS STILL SIN

There can be a number of reasons why we as Christians still sin. One of those reasons is not because it is in our nature to do so. Paul says we are now "slaves of righteousness" because we have been set free from the taskmaster of sin (Romans 6:18). We sin because we choose to, not because we are prone to it in our hearts. The pharaoh of sin has been drowned in the Red Sea of baptism in Christ. He is condemned and dead forever!

Adam and Eve did not have a sin nature and yet they made a choice to disobey God. The devil presented a lie to them, and they took the bait. The devil did not force them into anything. He simply made a sales pitch and they paid for it! The bottom line is, Adam and Eve made a choice. This tells us two very important things. The first thing is God empowers us with the dignity to make powerful life choices. The second thing is at the root of every act of sin is a lie. Usually it's a lie concerning the nature of God and our identity. These are the two biggest battlefields of the mind for the believer. This is why it is so important to remain in the truth and to remind ourselves of what God declares over us. We need to daily be intentional and focused with renewing our minds with God's truth. "I cannot afford to have a thought in my head that is not in His" (Bill Johnson). It's important for us to think and believe like God. This is the process of transformation that we are all in (Romans 12:2).

We still have the power to make a choice no matter what the lie or the circumstance is. We must take responsibility for our choices. Usually the blame game starts after we have made wrong choices, as it was with Adam and Eve. They both blamed each other when God was questioning them about their choice to disobey. Nothing has the power to make you sin but you. This is why repentance is so important in our initial response to the gospel and in the process of transformation in our relationship with God. The word "repentance" in the Greek means to "change the way you think." That's why everywhere Jesus went, He would say, "Repent! For the kingdom of heaven is at hand." As we read in the gospels, many rejected Him because they refused to change the way they were thinking. They remained in their sins because of pride and deception. They loved lies more than the truth!

I am fully convinced that the struggle with sin for most of us is due to holding on to wrong concepts and lies about God and about our identity and worth. The solution is in the renewing of the mind. Sometimes a person may need deliverance or emotional healing, but in my experience even these issues are almost always tied to lies and wrong thinking. We can go through deliverance session after deliverance session, but if our mind isn't renewed to the truth then we won't find the empowerment to walk in consistent victory. Strongholds form out of a wrong belief system.

Jesus said, "If you abide in my word, you are truly my disciples, and you will know the truth, and the truth will set you free" (John 8:31–32). The key is remaining, meditating on, and digesting His word. This is where the lies we are believing get replaced with the truth. The result is living in the freedom of the sons and daughters of God. "So if the Son sets you free, you will be free indeed" (John 8:36). We are already free in Christ. Our mind is in the process of believing the truth of this reality in every aspect of our lives. *So the issue is in our believing, not in a sin nature residing in us!* We need to ask ourselves what we are believing and why. What voice are we listening to? The father of lies or the Father of lights? We are enabled to discern between these two voices and to say no to the lie and yes to the truth. God's voice will always lead us into greater levels of freedom in every area of our lives.

THE MYSTERY

The mystery is we are a new creation in the present tense and yet at the same time we are being transformed by the renewing of our minds (Romans 12:1–2). It is important to embrace the work of transformation God has already done and the work of transformation He is in the process of doing every day of our lives. We are living in this tension constantly. The renewed mind is when our thinking is in agreement with the mind of Christ (2 Corinthians 2:16). Knowing the truth and believing like Jesus is the key to living in victory and freedom in every part of our lives.

> *"There is a difference between believing in Jesus and believing like Jesus. Our Lord told those "who believed in Him" that they needed to "know the truth" in order to be free in their life experience. Knowing the truth leads us to believe like Jesus" (Steve Backlund, Victorious Mindsets).*

As we intimately come to know the truth, then we will easily detect lies. This is the weapon Jesus used in the wilderness in Matthew 4. He was so acquainted with the truth of the Word that the lie was easily detected. As sons and daughters, we have authority over lies and darkness. He wants us to be so rooted in the truth of who we are in Christ and the purpose of our lives that fleeting thoughts and lies become laughable.

HITTING THE TARGET

One of the root meanings for the word "sin" in the Greek is to "miss the mark." Think of it in terms of archery. When we are living in the truth of our identity in Christ, we are hitting the bull's-eye. With right believing, we will hit the mark. When we choose to believe the lie of sin, we are simply forgetting who we are and our new nature in Christ. In this case, we are missing the mark. The good news is Jesus has given us a Helper in this process. The Holy Spirit is actually with us as our Helper and Friend to constantly remind us of our new nature and who we are in Christ. He is called the Spirit of truth and He guides us into all truth. Not just some truth—all truth! One of His job descriptions is to convict us of righteousness (John 16:8–13). One of the root meanings of convict in the Greek is the word "convince." The Holy Spirit works to convince us of our new nature and identity in Christ, and of the righteousness of God in us. We need the Holy Spirit's empowerment in our lives as He declares to us what the Father declares over us.

Some think the Spirit's primary job description in our lives is to make us feel bad for our sins. This is actually a lower standard of thinking than what God intends for us. He is not here to help us manage our sin habits or to prevent us from doing bad things. He is here to lead us into all truth. He empowers us with a mindset of victory. This doesn't mean He won't ever convict us of sin choices that turn into destructive behavior. He will convict us in order to remind us of who we are in Christ and to lead us into freedom. It's the kindness of God that leads us to repent or change the way we think. Condemnation is the exact opposite. It's like bathing in a mud puddle. You end up feeling dirty and hopeless in your sins. Conviction, on the other hand, leads us to the solution to our problems.

If we do miss the mark and choose to sin, we need to own it and ask for forgiveness. "If we confess our sins, He is faithful and just to forgive us our sins and to cleanse us from all unrighteousness" (1 John 1:9). Owning and confessing our sin choices to God positions us to receive greater levels of mercy and grace. Mercy is receiving forgiveness and cleansing from unrighteousness when we deserve punishment. Grace is the empowerment to walk in personal victory over familiar sin habits. God is continually abounding and overflowing in mercy and grace!

The more we make right choices over a particular temptation in the empowerment of grace, the more we grow in authority to set others free who are entangled in that same area. Again, grace does not make allowance for sin to remain in our lives. We are designed to live in the light. Anything kept hidden or in the dark becomes a foothold or a doorway for the enemy to oppress us. To keep something in the dark is a direct violation of our original design. Since God is pure light and we were made in His image, it is only natural for us to also live in the light.

King David quickly owned his sin and repented when the prophet Nathan confronted him about his sin with Bathsheba. King Saul, on the other hand, was quick to make excuses and protect himself and his reputation when the prophet Samuel confronted him about his disobedience. David's top priority was his relationship with God and staying surrendered to Him. Any part of me that is not surrendered to the Lordship of Christ is still conformed to the mindset and pattern of this world. True repentance leads us to think differently and to have a different perspective on our approach to life. The result is we begin to live differently as we learn to think like God. It is impossible for God to have a hopeless or powerless thought in His mind. Let's learn to let His mind influence ours. We will then see our actions catch up with our beliefs.

We get to say yes to manifesting righteousness. We get to say yes to the Holy Spirit leading and empowering us to hit the target in our everyday life. He brings the best out in us. Not the worst! It's actually in our nature now to hit the mark in life as beloved sons and daughters of God. If we do miss the mark, we have a good King who will never reject us or withhold His love and forgiveness. We can run to Him with honesty and humility because there is nothing His love can't handle (1 John 2:1-2). Believing the truth and remaining in the unconditional love of the Father gives us this confidence.

BREAKING STRONGHOLDS

Lies only have power when they are agreed with and acted upon. We were designed to empower whatever we put our faith in, and sometimes we put our faith in the wrong thing. This is how strongholds are formed that lead to negative behavior and even the breakdown of relationships in our lives. Truth always has the power to break the lie!

Several years ago, I made the decision to go back and hang out with some of my drinking buddies for a night. We started out in the bar, playing pool and drinking a few beers. I began to rationalize it by telling myself I wasn't drunk and I was trying to be a light to my friends. The truth of the matter is I was hurting inside and was really feeling like a failure. I was looking for an escape from what I was feeling. I believed the lie that I was a screw-up and believed drinking alcohol would somehow numb my pain. My belief system wasn't working out too well for me!

After the bar, I went to my friend's house and kept drinking. I was completely drunk as the night went on. I began to preach the gospel to my friends and made a fool out of myself. At one point I went to the bathroom and was staring at myself in the mirror. In that moment, I heard the Lord ask me a question as clear as day: "What are you doing here?" I knew His question was not for His sake; it was for me. I then heard Him say, "I love you, son!" I was instantly cut right to the heart and began to cry. It was knowing how much He loved me that pierced my heart. I was so grieved and filled with sorrow. It was as if He was saying, "Remember My love for you and who you belong to. This is not who you are!" I came out of the bathroom and told my friends I had to leave. I went back to my dad's house and went right to the bathroom to throw up. My dad came in because he heard me getting sick and began rubbing my back. I kept telling him over and over, "I am such a screw up! I am such a screw up!" He kept telling me that wasn't true and that he was proud of me. Out of my own mouth came the root issue—the kingpin lie. It wasn't a sin nature that led me helplessly into that foolish night of drinking. That line of thinking is completely powerless. It was a deep-rooted lie I believed about myself that led me to make some bad choices. I had a sabotaging belief that no matter how good things got in my life, I would somehow screw it up. I didn't realize that this thinking would manifest even when I was doing well in life. It was as if I needed to create a problem in order to let myself off the hook from the pressure of living for God. I knew God had called me to greatness and wanted to give me favor and influence, but it scared me big time! This was primarily because I was relying upon myself to make it happen. It took the power of the truth and God's extravagant love to uproot this vicious lie.

After I owned some things with the Lord the next day, I went to each of my friends who were there the previous night and asked for forgiveness for not living according to my convictions. I cleaned up my mess. The issue for me wasn't just forgiveness. I knew God was good and that He would forgive me. The issue for me was genuine repentance that led to a changed life. The lies needed to be replaced with the truth. My mind was being renewed so I could live an empowered life that reflected the true nature of grace at work in me. I can say that I am free today of this vicious lie because I know how loved and accepted I am in Papa God's love. I know that I am more than a conqueror through Christ who loves me. God does not despise us in the process of transformation; He loves us even when it gets a little messy! There is always hope for every broken part of our lives.

THE BEST YOU!

"This I say, therefore, and testify in the Lord, that you should no longer walk as the rest of the Gentiles walk, in the futility [perverse and void of truth] of their mind, having their understanding darkened, being alienated from the life of God… That you put off, concerning your former conduct, [way of living] the old man which grows corrupt according to the deceitful lusts, and be renewed in the spirit of your mind, and that you put on the new man which was created according to God, in true righteousness and holiness" (Ephesians 4: 17–18a, 22–24).

The old perverse way of thinking and living is not who we are anymore! The "old man" is to be put off or shed like an old pair of stained clothes, and we are to put on "the new man." The new man is wrapped up and hidden in Christ Himself. In Him, we are empowered to live a life of true righteousness and holiness. Jesus brings out the best you to shine forth. You are not called to be anyone else. He wants you to be free to be you. This process of transformation happens in the environment of His pursuing love. He causes us to be fully alive in His loving presence! We are no longer void of truth. We are a new creation and are now prone to righteousness through the empowerment (or grace) of God. Paul's instruction to "Be renewed in the spirit of your mind ..." indicates the key to living out the best you. The "spirit" of the mind includes our attitude, feelings, decision making, etc. The truth even sets our feelings free and gives us the ability to make great decisions. I would encourage you to read through your Bible and begin to highlight the places where it declares who you are in Christ. Write down what you find, and declare it over yourself daily with joy. Declarations simply align our thinking and the course of our lives with the truth of God and what He promises us in scripture.

> *"If then you were raised with Christ, seek those things which are above, where Christ is, sitting at the right hand of God. Set your mind on things above, not on things on the earth. For you died, and your life is hidden with Christ in God (Colossians 3:1–3).*

QUESTIONS:

- What would the result be of primarily focusing on trying to fix or manage our dead sin nature? Does the truth that you are free from the taskmaster of sin change the focus of your life? How does this change what you declare about yourself?

- Is the truth that you have a new nature and that you are now prone to righteousness a revolutionary mindset change for you? How are you already living in new creation reality?

- Are there any lies you believe about your identity as a follower of Jesus? What truth is your heavenly Father replacing those lies with?

DECLARATIONS:

- I am a new creation. I am dead to sin and now prone to righteousness!
- I am being transformed by the renewing of my mind. I have the mind of Christ!
- I am walking in purity and purpose. I have a great destiny!
- I am no longer a sinner—I am a saint. Jesus is bringing out the best me!

ACTIVATIONS:

- Spend time with God and ask Him for specific truths in His Word He is highlighting in this season of your life. Write them down if you need to. Let these truths renew you in the spirit of your mind. Feast on these truths and declare them out daily. This is who you are and what you were born for. You are accepted and delighted in!

- Take some time to thank God for giving you the Helper—the Spirit of truth. Thank you, Father, that we are not left as orphans! Invite the Holy Spirit to be the strongest voice in your life as He helps you continue to victoriously destroy lies and to hit the mark of your new creation identity. Invite Him to bring out the best you and see how your interactions with people improve for the positive.

CHAPTER NINE

New Creation Heart

*"Then I will sprinkle clean water on you, and you shall be clean; I will cleanse you from all your filthiness and from all your idols. **I will give you a new heart and put a new spirit within you**; I will take the heart of stone out of your flesh and give you a heart of flesh. I will put My Spirit within you and cause you to walk in My statutes ..." (Ezekiel 36:25–27a).*

The moment God's love got a hold of us at salvation, we were given a brand new heart and a new spirit. He does not fix our old heart that is stained and tattered by sin. He has no intentions of helping us manage a heart prone to sin! He takes that old heart which was deceitful and "desperately wicked" and He removes it from within us (Jeremiah 17:9). This verse out of Jeremiah is describing a heart still ruled by sin. Many have used this verse to prove that our hearts will always be prone to sin—that we will some how always be led astray because our hearts are deceitful. For the born-again child of God, this is simply not true. Check out the language Paul uses in Romans to describe what God does with our old heart that was prone to sin.

"But he is a Jew who is one inwardly; and circumcision is that of the heart, in the Spirit, not in the letter, whose praise is not from men but from God" (Romans 2:29).

Your old hardened and rebellious heart has been crucified with Christ and is dead. Even more graphic than that, Paul says your old heart is circumcised and cut away the second the Holy Spirit fills it. God purchased your corrupted heart with the high price of His Son's blood. He took it away and does not plan on giving it back! He purchased a new heart for each one of us. All that is required is that we believe. Christ alone accomplished this glorious work. Something instantaneous takes place when the Spirit of God comes to live inside of us. We become a new creation altogether. This is a beautiful work of grace.

GOD-FILLED HEART

The new heart you have been given has the ability to be so filled with God Himself that you cannot contain Him spilling out of you. It is a heart created by God and created for God Himself. It is the place where the Holy Spirit now dwells. It is the place where we enjoy unbroken union with our Creator.

I have really good news for you: You don't have to work hard anymore at trying to fix your old wicked heart that once was prone to sin. He already did it for you to the glory of His praise. He gave you a new heart so He can commune with you. He doesn't want your performance. He wants you! The goal of the Christian is to know God and to be so full of Him that we are brimming over in all of life. We now have a new creation heart in Christ. We can now draw near to God's holy presence without fear. Not only that, He can also draw near to us. Better yet, He now lives inside of us. The fullness of God dwells in Christ, and Christ dwells in us. We are complete in Him.

"Beware lest anyone cheat you through philosophy and empty deceit, according to the tradition of men, according to the basic principles of the world, and not according to Christ. For in Him dwells all the fullness of the Godhead bodily; and you are complete in Him, who is the head of all principality and

power. In Him you were also circumcised with the circumcision made without hands, by putting off the body of the sins of the flesh, by the circumcision of Christ, buried with Him in baptism, in which you also were raised with Him through faith in the working of God, who raised Him from the dead" (Colossians 2:8–12).

LIVING FROM THE OVERFLOW

I was out on the streets in the Tenderloin District of San Francisco with the assignment to bring light into darkness through love. The Tenderloin District is a dangerous place full of public drug use, male and female prostitution, gang violence, and a high level of intense spiritual activity. My friend and I sat right next to a couple of guys who were sitting on the sidewalk in a rough area with lots of drugs. We were pretty sure they had already been using or were about to use drugs. We tried to connect with them initially, but they didn't seem to want to talk a whole lot. So we just sat there and prayed quietly, believing God wanted to do something simply because He loved them. After a short time of this awkward silence, one of the guys stood up abruptly and said, "I need to get out of here and go up to my room and read my Bible!" We tried to reach out to him, but he quickly took off. He was very genuine and seemed to be convicted as we were sitting next to him.

After that experience, I realized the Holy Spirit was working on his heart from the overflow of our lives being filled with God's presence. We didn't even need to say much at all. When you know who you are in Christ and live from the reality that your heart is God-filled, then people will be changed just by being near you. The Holy Spirit rests upon you in power. You change the spiritual atmosphere everywhere you go just by being you and by living intentionally in His extravagant love.

TENDING TO THE GARDEN OF OUR HEART

I like to think of my heart as a garden. One of the responsibilities God gave Adam and Eve was to tend to and care for the Garden of Eden. The

Garden of Eden was the perfect paradise and yet it could become over-grown if it was not taken care of properly. This is an amazing revelation of God's character. He creates something perfect and beautiful, yet He does not remove our responsibility or our ability to make choices from the equation. He empowers us to tend to and care for what He created from scratch. God does not remove our humanity from His plans and purposes in the world. This is a beautiful partnership with Him. God does not want robots. He wants mature sons and daughters of God who learn to make decisions from love in every aspect of life.

We still have the power and dignity to choose what is highest and best for our heart. We can also allow weeds to grow in the garden of our heart if we are not being diligent to keep it soft and yielded to the love and mercy of God. I'm talking about weeds such as bitterness, jealousy, envy, pride, unforgiveness, lust, etc. These weeds become a perversion at work in our heart and begin to manifest in our attitudes and actions if left unchecked and undealt with. They can cause a perversion to our true identity as redeemed sons and daughters. The best of us does not come out in life when weeds are allowed to take root and grow. This can be one of the problems with a lifestyle of busyness, even in ministry! Busyness does not equal fruitfulness. Fruitfulness comes from inti-macy with Christ. It comes from remaining and abiding in Him and contin-ually receiving nourishment from His Spirit. It is our responsibility to guard over our heart with all diligence. "Keep your heart with all diligence, for out of it spring the issues of life" (Proverbs 4:23).

PRACTICAL WAYS TO TEND TO OUR HEART

Our heart is the source and spring of every part of our life. Whatever is going on internally will affect our attitude, perspective, words, and actions. Our internal world will affect the world around us, positively or negatively. God has given us the tools to tend to our heart successfully. Here are four practical things that have helped me in my journey with God:

1. Remaining passionately in love with Jesus. We were created first for love. Keeping ourselves in the love of God as passionate worshipers gives no room or space for weeds to take root and grow in our heart. The fire of His love burns it all out! There is no need to watch over our heart with fear or anxiety. We don't need to go "naval diving" for something wrong or sinful. Just gaze upon the face of Jesus and intentionally live a life of gratitude and adoration. The passionate pursuit of His face is the goal. We are not called to just obey God and work for Him; we are called to love Him and be loved by Him. This is the place where we learn to live from the abundance of a heart filled with Him.

Practical application: Take time to daily gaze upon God's beauty through worship/soaking and quality time with Him. Keep your heart yielded to Him in the secret place. Living a lifestyle of thanksgiving and adoration keeps us from a mindset of entitlement. Drink your fill of Christ's love and then give it away to others.

2. Meditating on the truth and declaring it. There is something powerful about taking time to digest the Word of God until it changes us. The Word of God is truth and the truth sets us free. It's not enough to get in the Word—we need the Word to get into us so much that our minds are renewed to think like God. We cannot allow our negative experiences to dictate what we believe if we want to see transformation. Our beliefs, rooted in the Word of God, need to dictate how we respond to our life experiences. We can easily detect lies as we learn to submit our minds to the truth. A powerful way to be transformed by the renewing of our minds is by declaring the truth. Declaring the truth aligns us with heaven. Our declarations need to be rooted in faith, not feelings. This keeps our perspective filled with hope as we choose victorious mindsets.

Practical application: Invite the Holy Spirit into your Bible reading. Chew on the Word until God speaks to you. Ask Him to renew your mind and fill your heart with truth. Invite the sword of His Word to help you discern between a belief rooted in a lie and a belief rooted in truth. Take time then to declare boldly the promises of God over your life and over others. Your declarations make a difference!

3. Paying attention to our attitude toward others. Our attitude toward others is a good indicator of what's going on in our heart, positive or negative. Of course we don't want to wait until wrong attitudes come up to care for our heart. Sometimes we get busy and neglect the most important part of our lives. The key is staying full of the Spirit so the fruit of love is evident. If we are getting irritable with others, it is a clear sign that something is off in our perspective. We are not seeing life or responding to life according to our new creation identity in Christ. Love is the greatest fruit of the Spirit and if we are lacking in that department, then something needs to be re-calibrated in our thinking or uprooted from our heart. The true mark of spirituality is not in how many miracle breakthroughs we are seeing but in how we are treating others.

Practical application: Take some time to step away from the busyness of life and ask the Holy Spirit to help you make the proper adjustments in your thinking or in your heart. For me, sometimes it is as simple as taking time to rest or doing something recreational if I've been neglecting that part of my life. Learn to love and care for yourself the way God loves and cares for you. The best of us comes out to benefit others when we love and care for ourselves. Laugh a lot and don't take life too seriously. "A joyful heart is good medicine, but a crushed spirit dries up the bones" (Proverbs 17:22). This is key to our health and longevity.

4. Staying accountable to others in community. Giving people permission to speak into our lives and to challenge us is a key to staying healthy. Nobody is meant to be isolated when walking through life's issues. Maintaining openness and honesty with God and others will prevent weeds from sprouting up. This keeps us safe and undeceived. It is important that we don't try to cover things up. An attempt at being a strong Christian in our own strength can be a hindrance to the freedom Jesus intends for us. It takes courage to be open and honest. It takes courage to live in the light in the context of healthy relationships. Things kept in the dark will only lead us into shame and isolation. As we walk in the light, we maintain healthy fellowship with God and with others in the body of Christ.

Practical application: Join a community of believers who highly value family and commit to doing life with them. Consider joining a small group or a home group. Grow in relationship with other healthy people, and invite them to speak into your life. Healthy people don't tear you down; they build you up and challenge you to greatness.

SANCTIFICATION IS A PERSON

"But God has chosen the foolish things of the world to put to shame the wise, and God has chosen the weak things of the world to put to shame the things which are mighty; and the base things of the world and the things which are despised God has chosen, and the things which are not, to bring to nothing the things that are, that no flesh should glory in His presence. But of Him you are in Christ Jesus, who became for us wisdom from God – and righteousness and sanctification and redemption – that, as it is written, 'He who glories, let him glory in the LORD'" (1 Corinthians 1:27–31).

The word "sanctification" means to be "set apart" or "consecrated to God." According to Paul, to be set apart and consecrated is found "in Christ Jesus." It's not a personal virtue based on obedience or good works. Good works are the result of being set apart. The traditional concept is justification is instant, while sanctification is a process. Paul describes righteousness and sanctification as being found in a Person—Jesus Christ. Jesus Christ Himself has become our sanctification. We are set apart and made holy in Him alone. The goal is to depend upon and abide in Him rather than depending on our own efforts or theology. Sanctification is not a process based on our disciplines and efforts to become holy. Paul is painfully clear to those who want to work their way into holiness—let no human effort glory in what only the Lord Himself produces in us. We are "in Christ" the Holy One, and He is in us. You can't get any more sanctified or set apart than that.

This of course does not give us a license to sin and be irresponsible in our behavior and interactions with people just because we are already set apart in Him. On the contrary, we honor our heart connection with God and others because we have been sanctified and set apart in Christ. The fruit of being set apart in Christ is knowing Him and displaying His heart to others. I am set apart for a purpose, not to boast and be rude about my theology, but to display the character of Christ and represent Him well to the world around me.

There is a process to being transformed by the renewing of our minds and to the character of Christ being worked into our lives. I also believe there can be a process for emotional healing due to trauma, oppression, abuse, etc. These realities are also a work of grace found in the person of Jesus. Whether it's an instant work already accomplished or a process, we are dependent upon the grace of God found only in Jesus and His finished works on the cross. Our only requirement in the process is to believe the truth and keep a big YES in our heart to His divine influence. By grace we are now living from sanctification, not for it.

SANCTIFIED IMAGINATION

The truth that we are already sanctified in Christ is very freeing. To know that I have a sanctified imagination and my heart is not evil is empowering. If

I believe I am evil or any part of my life is still evil, it's going to be really difficult to live in the abundant life promised in Christ. This way of thinking leads only to a life of struggle and defeat. Jesus has defeated sin and re-created us to live in Him and to know His voice in our everyday life. Even our imagination has been made clean and set apart. Think of our imagination like being a pure white canvas the Holy Spirit can paint upon. Wow! God has joined His Spirit to our spirit (1 Corinthians 6:17). The thoughts and beauty of God's heart can be painted upon the canvas of our imagination as we stay in rhythm with Him. Because of this, we can know the depths of God's heart and mind, and then display what we have seen and heard to the world around us. His desire is to express His creative nature through the vehicle of our imagination as we learn to partner with Him.

Some say our imagination is "the devil's playground." How can this be true when we are a new creation? Adam and Eve were created with an imagination before sin came into the world. All it takes is one word articulated in a certain way and our imagination takes off and begins to create worlds! God created us with this childlike ability to reveal His glory in creative ways. It stands to reason that God has an imagination and uses it since we are created in His image. Again, the key to all of this is remaining yielded to the influence of the Holy Spirit upon our lives. Living yielded is not hard, nor is it full of self-effort. It is a place of rest and childlikeness. Asking, "What are You doing today, Papa?" becomes the focus rather than gritting our teeth to fight off sin, the world, and the devil. What a place of joy and freedom of expression!

THE CROWN AND THE FLOWER

My wife and I were at a revival service one night and she went up front for prayer at the end of the service. She was in need of encouragement since we had gone through around three years of difficulty with having our second child. We had recently experienced loss and grief before we were at this particular service, and we needed to hear from Papa God. A young woman on the ministry team gave my wife a simple but amazing word. She told Jenny she saw the Lord placing a crown on her head and He gave her a flower. He was saying to Jenny, "Thank you for trusting Me! You are doing a great job." Of course we knew what that meant, and we were both very encouraged by that word.

A day or two later my daughter, Jasmine, who was six years old at the time, drew a picture on a napkin. She gave it to Jenny and told her Jesus had shown her what to draw. My wife looked at the napkin, and it was a picture of a crown and a flower! We were completely blown away by this because we had not shared with Jasmine the word Jenny received a couple nights before. The Lord showed our daughter the exact same thing He showed the young woman on the ministry team. Her imagination became the canvas the Holy Spirit could paint upon to communicate His heart again to Jenny. What a good God!

NEW CREATION LENSES

> *"For the love of Christ compels us, because we judge thus: that if One died for all, then all died; and He died for all, that those who live should live no longer for themselves, but for Him who died for them and rose again. Therefore, from now on, we regard no one according to the flesh. Even though we have known Christ according to the flesh, yet now we know Him thus no longer" (2 Corinthians 5:14–16).*

Just as important as agreeing with the truth about ourselves, is our ability to see others through the eyes of Christ and His accomplished works on the cross. I found it too easy in my own life to stumble over the weaknesses and flaws I saw in others. I quickly called a criticizing attitude "the gift of discernment." I have learned over the years that it doesn't take a spiritual gift to see what is wrong with others, but it does take faith to see Christ in others. Paul exhorts us, in view of the completed works of Christ on the cross, to "regard no one according to the flesh." So if we are not to perceive others according to the natural, then how are we to perceive them? We are to perceive others by the Spirit—through new creation lenses! Paul is often making a contrast in his letters between what is natural (the flesh) and the life of the Spirit. It's only through the influence of the Spirit in our life that we can rightfully perceive people and honor who they are in Christ. If I believe that Christ died in my place to make me a brand new creation, then I also must believe He has done this in others. This is the only way we can truly honor one another. God gives us the ability to perceive others based upon His work of grace in their lives. Nobody is perfect in the body of Christ, or the world for that matter. We all have "stuff" in our lives that is being worked out as we are being transformed by the renewing of our minds and learning to walk in the wholeness Christ paid for. I am learning to be gracious and to recognize the positive growth happening in others. This takes intentionality on my part. It starts with adjusting my focus to the "blooming flower" and not to the thorns in people's lives. Honor is the ability to celebrate a person's life without stumbling over their weaknesses and shortcomings. Life flows through honor! It's the first command with a promise.

> *"Honor your father and your mother, that your days may be long in the land that the LORD your God is giving you"* *(Exodus 20:12).*

It starts with us giving honor rather than expecting it! I truly believe honor from a genuine heart is the key to a sustained outpouring and movement of the Spirit in the earth. How we treat one another and handle conflict in the Body of Christ will either quench the Spirit or add fuel to what He is doing. Treating others with familiarity blinds us from seeing the potential and greatness in others. It is a killer to the anointing and life of the Spirit freely flowing through our lives. It will always lead to dishonor, and dishonor always quenches the Spirit. Treating one another with love and honor actually honors what Christ did on the cross. He paid such a high price to forgive us and set us free from sin. His love is generous, and it delights the Father's heart when we love one another the way He loves us. The Spirit produces love and honor, and He is also greatly attracted to it. Authentic love and honor reveal to the world what Jesus is like! "Love one another with brotherly affection. Outdo one another in showing honor" (Romans 12:10).

We are actually given permission to compete and outdo one another in showing honor. Notice how it doesn't say to outdo one another in receiving honor! Jesus clearly confronted the Pharisees and religious leaders of His day because they positioned themselves in a place to be honored by men rather than modeling it toward others. Let's ask God for the ability to see others "in Christ" without stumbling over their weaknesses. This does not mean we won't ever have conflict. It just means we will be committed to handling conflict with a high level of love and honor. Maintaining healthy connections is the priority in an honoring culture. We have been empowered into new creation reality with the ability to perceive and treat others the way Jesus perceives and treats them. The fruit of living in our new creation identity will be clearly seen in how we treat others. This is absolutely crucial when it comes to our mission to see the world around us transformed with the gospel of grace.

QUESTIONS:

- How does the truth that your heart is not evil impact you? What are the things you do to care for your heart and to keep it overflowing with God?
- Does the truth that Jesus Himself is your sanctification change the way you view or approach holiness? How has the Holy Spirit worked through your imagination to reveal Himself to you or to others?
- Have you thought of honoring and seeing others through the eyes of Christ as fruit of the God-filled heart? From your perspective, what is the good fruit of a person living in new creation reality?

DECLARATIONS:

- I have a new creation heart in Christ. My heart was made to be God-filled!
- My heart and my imagination are sanctified. I co-create with the Holy Spirit!
- I hear from God more than I think I do. I see others through the lenses of the cross!

ACTIVATIONS:

- Imagine yourself climbing into Father God's lap. Remember, you have access to His throne as a delighted in child. How do you view God when He looks at you? What do you see in His eyes? What is He saying to you? Write these things down in a journal and remind yourself of the Father's heart for you frequently.
- Drink your fill of His intoxicating love and presence, full of thanksgiving!
- Ask the Father to give you His eyes to see others the way He sees them. As we are tracking with the Father's heart, He empowers us to view and treat others according to the Spirit. Set your mind to love and honor people the way God would love and honor them in your family, workplace, and in your community. Partner with the Holy Spirit in this with joy. Have fun!

Grace Empowers

CHAPTER TEN

Living in Rhythm with the Spirit

"There is now no condemnation for those who are in Christ Jesus. For the law of the Spirit of life has set you free in Christ Jesus from the law of sin and death. For God has done what the law, weakened by the flesh, could not do. By sending His own Son in the likeness of sinful flesh and for sin, He condemned sin in the flesh, in order that the righteous requirement of the law might be fulfilled in us, who walk not according to the flesh but according to the Spirit" (Romans 8:1–4).

We are now empowered to live in rhythm with the Spirit because the taskmaster of sin has been condemned and removed from our lives. We have been set free from the law of sin and death. Jesus has come to live on the inside of us through the life and power of His Spirit. The flesh is the sinful nature that is opposed to God. The flesh also speaks of living by our own human efforts or willpower to get God's approval. This is no longer our identity. The righteous requirements of the law are now fulfilled in us as we live our lives in the Spirit. Living in rhythm with the Spirit is true freedom for God's cherished and empowered sons and daughters. The Spirit always empowers us with the

Father's love. I have found that love in action is always the evidence of a life truly filled with and led by the Spirit. The following is an example of what this looks like in my life.

I was at a mall in Ohio with my family, enjoying a day off. I ended up waiting outside the restroom for my wife and daughters with my three-year-old son, Judah. While I was waiting, I became very aware of the goodness of God's presence in an increasing measure. I love His presence! In these moments, I listen to what He is saying and look for what He is doing. I then noticed a woman in a wheelchair having a difficult time getting the door open to the entrance of the mall. I was moved with compassion for her, so I took my son with me to open the door for her. I introduced myself and Judah and asked her how we could pray for her. I noticed she had a wrap around one of her feet. She said she was possibly going to lose her foot due to an extreme case of diabetes. Right at the moment when we were talking about her foot, Judah reached out and touched the wrap on her foot. I knew He was flowing in the Spirit along with me. We declared a brand new pancreas and a life free of diabetes. We also released the goodness of God on her foot for healing. As we were praying, I was getting words for her that were right out of the heart of the Father.

We told her she is a treasure and so loved by God. As I was speaking these things over her, she began to wipe away her tears. The love of God was clearly breaking in! Judah and I didn't see her get instantly healed in that moment, but we knew God was touching her life in a dramatic way and I was confident that healing got released to her body. It's impossible to pray with child-like faith and not have anything happen. God shows up every time we pray because of love! Loving others and releasing God's presence is as natural as breathing when we stay in rhythm with Him. It's all in staying connected to God's heart. For me, this all flows out of cultivating relationship with the Holy Spirit and learning to enjoy Him in all of life.

YOU MUST BE BORN AGAIN

Being born again is the beginning point to developing relationship with the Spirit. The foundation of being born of the Spirit is central to the gospel.

Some teachings have muddied these waters and have brought confusion to some in the body of Christ. Let's go to the plumb line of truth and see what the Bible teaches about being born again.

> *"You, however, are not in the flesh but in the Spirit, if in fact the Spirit of God dwells in you. Anyone who does not have the Spirit of Christ does not belong to Him" (Romans 8:9).*

This is about as clear and as simple as it gets. Anyone who has the Spirit of Christ belongs to Him. Paul very clearly makes a contrast between those who belong to Christ and those who don't. Not everyone in the world is already born of the Spirit or belongs to Christ. Jesus Himself declares that a person must be born of the Spirit to enter the kingdom of God (John 3:3). This reality only happens at the confession of faith in response to the gospel (Romans 10: 8–11). We must believe to receive the free gift of righteousness and confess for salvation to be a reality in our lives. It is important for us to have this biblical foundation in our experience and in the way we present the good news to the world. With this truth in mind, I would like to address a theological stance that is growing popular in some circles known as the "Doctrine of Inclusion." This doctrine is rooted in the belief that all of humanity was already included in the death and resurrection of Christ over 2000 years ago, and we just need to convince them of this reality. According to this doctrine, somehow all of humanity is already mysteriously forgiven, reconciled, joined to the Spirit of God, and seated in union with Christ in heaven. This is based on 2 Corinthians 5:14–20.

Some believe that Paul is describing all of humanity dying with Christ in this passage of scripture rather than just those who believe. There are many arguments on both sides of this controversial belief. My goal is to explain why I think the Doctrine of Inclusion can be very harmful and then to point us back to relationship with the person of Jesus. Some say we are to just convince everyone they are already saved and included in Christ so they can live from that reality. I have one major concern with this approach to evangelism—it confuses people by pointing them to a theological position rather than to the person of Jesus. The goal of evangelism is to bring people into a dynamic and life-altering relationship with Papa God through faith in Jesus. We never hear of Jesus or the apostles approaching evangelism this way in the Bible. In fact, they call people to repent and believe the good news. I absolutely believe the Father sees people as they were created to be in His image, and we have the honor and privilege of declaring this truth to people who don't know Him yet. That being said, the truth still remains that they must be born of the Spirit by believing the gospel to be saved. Only then can a person truly belong to Christ and begin the process of being transformed by the renewing of their mind. To me, the Doctrine of Inclusion is dangerous because it's complicated and confuses people. It robs us of our ability to choose and somehow asserts that God secretly fills people with the Holy Spirit against their wishes. This is a ridiculous way of thinking. Again, it's about relationship, not a theological position. We get to say yes to God being in our lives. In my opinion, the Doctrine of Inclusion leads us into apathy and borderline unbelief. "If God already did everything, then I don't need to do a thing." This line of thinking slams the brakes on the great commission being fulfilled.

Is there any truth to the Doctrine of inclusion? The Bible teaches that redemption is a done deal because it is completely on God's side of the equation. Redemption is what He alone accomplished through Christ's sacrifice. We are already forgiven and somehow we were mysteriously joined with Christ at His death. Reconciliation, on the other hand, is not a done deal because reconciliation can only happen through the consent of two parties. God did His part on our behalf to reconcile us, and we need to do our part. If God takes away our part in the reconciliation, then God is not love. Love always empowers us to say yes or no. The good news is God isn't at odds with us. Before faith in Christ, we were all at odds with Him in our minds and in our actions. He already made peace with all of humanity through the cross. We just simply need to believe.

It is my conviction, based on the truth of Scripture, that the born-again experience becomes a reality at the point of believing and the confession of faith, not before. God joins His Spirit to ours at the point of saying yes to His invitation. He honors our choice and will not push Himself on us against our will. This is really good news!

IS HELL FOR REAL?

Here is another hot topic that needs to be addressed. Some believe hell is merely a state of mind or a present reality based on living in sin. The argument is "How can a God of love send people to hell?" The problem with this line of thinking is there is too much biblical support for an actual place called hell or "the lake of fire." Hell is a very real place (read Matthew 10:28, Luke 16:19–31, and Revelation 20:10–15). This is not something we are to celebrate or desire for anyone. At the same time, we cannot avoid its reality and create new theology simply because it doesn't seem to line up with what is acceptable in our society. God will one day remove everything that hinders love as the Judge of the earth. Everything He does is good and loving in nature, even as the Judge. To remove this aspect of God's character is to say we only like the parts of God that benefit us but not the part that establishes accountability and consequences. If we love Him, we must love all of Him!

Some go as far as believing every person will go to heaven whether they have a life-transforming, born-again experience or not. This has no biblical support and is a very dangerous belief system. Those who don't have the Spirit of Christ cannot please God, and the consequences of remaining in that mindset is eternal torment and separation from God's presence. Hell is a horrific consequence for those who choose to reject the One who designed them and the redemption He offers at the price of His Son's life. I truly believe the torment found in hell is the awareness of what a person could have experienced in Christ with the knowledge that they will never have it. This is not to be taken lightly in any way. Hell is not what God desires for any person, and we should never use hell to scare people into salvation. We know this to be true because God made provision for all of humanity to be saved through His Son's sacrifice. He desires that all would be saved and it's His kindness alone that leads people to repentance (Romans 2:4). Hell was designed for one being—the devil. All of humanity was designed for heaven. However, as I stated before, He has given all of humanity the dignity to receive this free gift or to reject it. We always have a choice because love is a choice. Our choices have consequences, either good or bad.

As the church, we cannot afford to adopt a man-centered gospel. The gospel must remain a Christ-centered gospel. Jesus paid too high of a price for it to come cheaply to people who couldn't care less. It is given to us completely free, and yet the gospel requires a decision to be made in order for a complete life change to take place. In this process of transformation, we die to what is opposed to God through the cross, and we are raised to life in Christ through resurrection. This is the pure gospel in its simplicity. We get to say yes to a complete life change and a dynamic relationship with a Person.

Some say that love will win out in the sense that everyone will go to heaven in the end no matter how they live or whether they believe the truth or not. But love from heaven is Christ centered, not self-centered. Love does not condone a lifestyle of sin and perversion. Love accepts us, transforms us on the inside and empowers us to be a living message to the world around us.

All of humanity is waiting to be born of the Spirit and we have the privilege of presenting this good news through love, service, and demonstrations of power. Jesus has already made provision for the whole world to be reconciled to the Father and to be instantaneously delivered from the domain of darkness. As we present God's heart to the world around us with love and honor, it will be really hard to pass up. The good news must remain the good news. Jesus died to take away the sins of the world and we have been given the ministry of reconciliation. Christ is, and must remain, at the center of this good news we preach and demonstrate. Relationship is the priority of the gospel.

CULTIVATING INTIMATE FRIENDSHIP

"The grace of the Lord Jesus Christ, and the love of God, and the fellowship of the Holy Spirit be with you all. Amen"
(2 Corinthians 13:14).

The word "fellowship" in this passage comes from the Greek word "koinonia." One of the root meanings of koinonia is to have a deep, intimate friendship. The fellowship of the Holy Spirit is to have an open, honest, and affectionate relationship with Him. The Holy Spirit is a Person and we have the privilege of getting to know Him personally. He has thoughts, feelings, and a will, just like the Father and the Son. It's important to understand that the Spirit is not just a force or an anointing we feel when we are in a setting of corporate worship or ministry. We have been invited into a dynamic, life-giving relationship with Him.

This relationship is without fear because the love of God has been poured into our hearts (Romans 5:5). God has come to live in our hearts and to take us deeper and deeper into the waters of His extravagant love and grace—into friendship. It can be too easy at times to confuse anointing and ministry success with relationship. We can make the mistake of only knowing the Spirit by what He gives us for ministry. At times we can even function in the gifts imparted to us and totally miss His heart. This happens by being motivated by ministry success instead of love. The gifts of the Spirit are meant to be an expression of God's nature—an expression of His love. They were not designed as methods just so we can get results. I never judge success by the amount of activity and results I am seeing. I judge success by the depth of intimate connection I have with the Father and my ability to express His heart to others. We were designed to know God. Everything else flows from this place of abiding. The more we cultivate friendship with the Spirit when no one is around or just in our day-to-day routines, the more we become sensitive to what He is saying and doing. We learn to move with His heartbeat because we love Him. We will see lasting fruit and kingdom breakthrough that glorifies the Father out of the priority of relationship.

At unplanned times, I will sense the slightest increase of the Holy Spirit's presence or prompting. Sometimes this happens when I am watching a movie or playing a game with my kids. I am learning to stop what I am doing even for a moment and just acknowledge His presence and spend time with my best Friend. Sometimes I initiate these moments of deeper connection and sometimes He does. Connection is the goal. It's not that He wants to take away something we are enjoying. He just simply loves to connect, sometimes at what seems like inconvenient times. No matter when or in what circumstance, it is our great honor and privilege to learn how to be sensitive to Him and respond for love's sake.

FILLED TO OVERFLOWING

"Therefore do not be foolish, but understand what the will of the Lord is. And do not get drunk with wine, for that is debauchery, but be filled with the Spirit, addressing one another in psalms and hymns and spiritual songs, singing and making melody to the Lord with your heart, giving thanks always and for everything to God the Father in the name of our Lord Jesus Christ, submitting to one another out of reverence for Christ" (Ephesians 5:17–21).

It is the will of God for us to be continually filled with the Holy Spirit. In fact, we were created for the fullness of God in every area of our lives. The will of God is easy. Spend time every day loving on God until you get so full that you can't help but spill out His goodness wherever you go. This is one aspect of what it means to love God and love others. Of course there are times when we don't feel a thing and love is purely a choice but we were ultimately designed to live from the overflow of a God-filled heart. It becomes as natural as breathing for us to give away what we have received in the secret place of God's heart. When Paul tells us to be filled with the Spirit, the understanding is that we would be liberally supplied and abounding to full measure! The Holy Spirit is a continual fountain inside of us. We are to drink our fill and then offer that drink to a parched and dying world. Oftentimes the church can also be parched and dying due to wrong concepts about what God requires from us. We think He cares more about our behavior and appearance rather than our heart. Sometimes we need to be reminded of the good news of a good God who is a continual fountain of abundant life. He simply requires that we keep ourselves in His love and stay completely full of Him. From this posture of heart, it becomes a joy to serve Him!

It has become a priority for me to posture my heart to continually receive so I can continue to overflow. The Spirit filling us is not a one-time encounter. Jesus gives the Spirit without measure. He broke the floodgates of heaven wide open at His sacrifice, and He doesn't plan on closing them. This is really good news because we now know what is available to us and what God desires. As we stay full and sensitive to how the Holy Spirit is moving, then others around us will experience His presence. According to Paul in the passage above, building others up, thankfulness, and a willingness to submit to and prefer others is evidence of a Spirit-filled life. Good fruit is the evidence of our lives overflowing with the Spirit. The way we treat others will give us long-term influence in our neighborhoods and cities. They must see this in our lives, not just in our talk.

FINDING OUR iPAD

Not too long ago, my wife and I were looking through our house for an iPad we couldn't find. We were trying to remember our steps from the last couple of days and where we saw the iPad last. We were worried that maybe we lost it. Instead of continuing to worry, my wife and ten-year-old daughter, Jasmine, decided to pray and ask Jesus where the iPad was. My daughter told me later that she jumped up and said to my wife, "I know where the iPad is!"

She explained how Jesus showed her a picture in her mind of the dresser in her room. In the picture, she saw the iPad under it. We have modeled for our kids as they grow up that Jesus will speak to us if we take the time to stop and listen, even if it is to find something we have lost in our home. Apparently Jasmine had more faith than we did in this circumstance. So, she ran into her room, looked under her dresser, and there she found the iPad just like Jesus showed her. Yay God! It was pretty awesome! What I love about this story is how it's a reminder that there is no junior Holy Spirit. The Spirit of God will speak to our children and lead us into the things He cares about and also into the things we care about. He is no respecter of persons. He is ready and eager to partner with whoever believes and has an open heart and mind to His leading. Like Jasmine, it just takes childlike faith and trust.

JOINT PARTICIPATION

"The grace of the Lord Jesus Christ, and the love of God, and the fellowship of the Holy Spirit be with you all. Amen" *(2 Corinthians 13:14).*

The other root meaning of the word "fellowship" (or koinonia) is "joint participation." This is also the same root meaning for "joint heir." Out of intimate connection, we learn to join with the Spirit in the Father's plans and purposes in the earth. We have the great privilege of seeing heaven's reality manifested in the earth by living in harmony with the Holy Spirit. With Him, we get to release righteousness and peace and joy everywhere we go! One of the greatest honors we have as the children of God is to participate in God's redemptive purposes. He could have done this whole thing by Himself—without you and me. But He didn't. He has not removed humanity from the equation. He loves to partner with us and invites us as joint heirs to play a key role in His will being done on earth as it is in heaven. This is astounding and humbling all at the same time. A good father wants his kids to join him in what he is accomplishing and exercises a tremendous amount of patience to do so. Why? It takes more time and interaction because it is done out of relationship rather than just giving orders. How much more does Father God have this grace and patience for us as we are learning to participate with Him in what He is doing? He has great patience even when we make mistakes in this learning process. As a result, His priority is not just obedience. It's learning to do life together from a place of intimacy. Lovers of God have privileges and insight into God's heart that casual seekers don't have! Casual seekers will not know the depths of God's heart. God is a "rewarder of those who diligently seek Him" (Hebrews 11:6). Every day can be an adventure with the Spirit. To know the Holy Spirit is to know the heart of God.

SET YOUR MIND ON THE SPIRIT

> *"For those who live according to the flesh set their minds on the things of the flesh, but those who live according to the Spirit set their minds on the things of the Spirit. For to set the mind on the flesh is death, but to set the mind on the Spirit is life and peace. You, however, are not in the flesh but in the Spirit, if in fact the Spirit of God dwells in you" (Romans 8:5–6, 9a).*

An important key to the Spirit-led life and living aware of what He is saying and doing starts with right believing. It starts by setting our mind on the things of the Spirit. This is both setting our mind on what the Scripture teaches us and on what the Spirit reveals to us. For me, this totally demystifies what it means to live according to the Spirit.

My concept for life in the Spirit for many years was not practical or simple in any way. I thought I had to live like some mystical monk off in the hills and then come out glowing with glory so the whole world would get saved. I separated my everyday life from what I considered to be "of the Spirit." I would hyper-spiritualize parts of my life, and not value what I deemed as "less spiritual." I am always expecting God to do unusual things that defy logic and reasoning, but the truth that I can simply set my mind on a target is simple and refreshing. It's empowering and not designated for "spiritual giants." Anyone can do this. The key is being very intentional about what we feed our minds with. "For as he thinks in his heart, so is he" (Proverbs 23:7a). We become or act out what we meditate on in our hearts and minds. The mind is a powerful tool when it is submitted to God. Others meditate to empty their mind. As followers of Jesus, we meditate to fill our minds with truth.

Some are waiting for God to just drop out of the sky, take over, and make all of their decisions for them. God is actually looking for lovers who will be intentional about setting their minds on Him and what He is doing in every aspect of their lives. To set my mind on the Spirit and what He is doing is not just designated for a scheduled devotional or Bible reading time. That's a good starting point, but Jesus died to be a part of our lives 24/7, not just for one hour a day! Let's not make the mistake of separating our God time from the rest of life.

The Holy Spirit wants to help us in the practical areas of life, just as much as He wants to partner with us to pull people up out of wheelchairs and raise the dead. The Spirit who inspired the book of Acts is the same Spirit who inspired Proverbs. Let's not compartmentalize what we perceive to be spiritual and non-spiritual. God is in all of life because God is in you! Being spiritual comes out of who we are and what we prioritize in our lives. The veil is torn. There is no separation between what is sacred and secular. "Christ in you, the hope of glory" (Colossians 1:27). Heaven and earth are connected and intertwined wherever we are, whether we are at work, the grocery store, or worshiping corporately at a church service. We are all empowered to take initiative and do our part. We can start each day with our mind set on God and an expectation of the life and activity of the Spirit throughout our day.

GROWING IN THE SPIRIT

These are three tools that helped me get to know the Holy Spirit and how to initiate partnership with Him:

1. A deep hunger to know God through His Word. What I find in the Scripture gives me a context for what I can expect of Him as I cultivate relationship. I found that I grow the most in discerning the voice of God and the leading of the Spirit when I am constantly filling my heart and mind with truth in the secret place. It's important to not just read the Bible as a religious duty. Expect to hear personally from God and to experience firsthand what you are meditating on. Let your Bible reading be a time of divine romance and fresh revelation. As we make this a priority, we will be quicker to discern His voice or His promptings in our everyday routines. We have a whole generation exposed to the supernatural these days, some good and some bad. The problem is, many don't know the Holy Spirit according to Scripture. Let's fall in love with the truth of God's Word and build from that solid foundation.

2. A passion to know God's heart in personal and corporate prayer. This is where I learned to align myself with His heart for others. It was in corporate times of prayer that I was sharpened to know His voice and His ways. I was able to bounce off others in the group what I was hearing and sensing. This is a safe place to excel in the things of the Spirit.

3. Taking risk with others in community. No one is meant to be isolated or to learn the ways of the Spirit on their own.

We were designed to grow together as a body. In community with other lovers of God and risk-takers is where we grow in a safe and a healthy environment. We naturally excel in these things by getting around others who are modeling joint participation and partnership with the Holy Spirit. Another person's breakthrough shows us what is possible. If I can see it in someone else's life, I can have it! The ways of the Spirit are more caught than taught.

GOD WORKS THROUGH NATURAL DESIRES

"For all who are led by the Spirit of God are sons of God. For you did not receive the spirit of slavery to fall back into fear, but you have received the Spirit of adoption as sons, by whom we cry, 'Abba! Father!'" (Romans 8:14–15).

I was on my way to work one morning, and I had a thought to go to Panera to work for a little bit on my computer before I went to the office. I was craving a good coffee for sure, but Panera was not the usual spot for me. I kind of wrestled with it at first, but then I decided to go to change things up a little. As I was walking up to the entrance of Panera, I saw a friend of mine waving at me through the window.

When I came in, he was excitedly telling me that God told him while he was driving that he would see me at Panera. He even saw an image of me walking up with my backpack, which is exactly what happened. Crazy! I hung out with him and his friend for a little bit and then after his friend left, he stayed to talk. There had been some conflict between us about six months prior to this, and we had forgiven each other and moved on, but had never restored the connection. I knew this was the right time for us to be open about the hurts from the past. It turned out to be an amazing time of healing and restoration for both of us. We actually have a stronger friendship now than we did before. Yay God!

I realized after what happened that this was a total God set up. The Spirit led me to Panera through my natural desire for coffee and a desire for a change of scenery that morning. I didn't hear a voice telling me to go to Panera and reconcile with my friend. Oftentimes I find the Spirit leading me through my natural desires. There is no separation between the natural and the Spirit realm. We are set apart and made one with Him, even in our desires.

It was also confirmed when my friend told me what God had revealed to him on his way to Panera. The fruit was obviously good. We just need to be open and expectant for Him to lead us in these ways. The Holy Spirit cares about every detail of our lives and is here to help and to guide us into a life of fruitfulness. If I claim to be "Spirit led" and yet the fruit of my life is constant conflict, an independent attitude, and strained relationships, I would question what spirit I am listening to. The fruit of the Spirit increasing in my life is the evidence of a Spirit-filled and Spirit-led life. Everything flows from and through love.

BORN INTO THE KINGDOM

"Truly, truly, I say to you, unless one is born again he cannot see the kingdom of God … Truly, truly, I say to you, unless one is born of water and the Spirit, he cannot enter the kingdom of God. That which is born of the flesh is flesh, and that which is born of the Spirit is spirit" (John 3:3, 5–6).

To be born of the Spirit is to live from a completely new operating system. The old is gone and the new has come! It is to live from a heart and mind filled with God Himself. It is the entry point into the reality of God's kingdom. Paul says, "He has delivered us from the domain of darkness and transferred us to the kingdom of His beloved Son, in whom we have redemption, the forgiveness of sins" (Colossians 1:13–14).

The instant you believed the gospel by turning to Jesus as your Savior and King, you entered into a brand new reality and received a new set of lenses. You entered the King's dominion. How is it that you can live in this world and yet live in the reality of the kingdom of God at the same time? It's because The kingdom of God is found in the person of the Holy Spirit and the manifestation of His presence and power flowing in and through our lives. "For the kingdom of God is not a matter of eating and drinking but of righteousness and peace and joy in the Holy Spirit" (Romans 14:17). The kingdom of God is the rule and reign of King Jesus being tangibly revealed. It will be physically manifested in fullness when Jesus physically returns to the earth. For now, it's important for us to understand the kingdom is an accessible realm within and all around us.

The kingdom is first within us by being filled with the Holy Spirit and cultivating relationship with Him. This is only possible through Jesus sitting as King in our heart. The kingdom is then manifested to the world around us as we stay in rhythm with the Spirit. Holy Spirit always seeks to establish and advance the rule and reign of King Jesus in the earth and we get to join Him!

We see this reality for the first time since Adam when Jesus blew on His disciples and said, "Receive the Holy Spirit" (John 20:21–23). Jesus breathed His Spirit into them, understanding that He was restoring mankind to his original place in God, which is to have dominion of the earth so God's kingdom would advance.

The Spirit living on the inside of us gives us the ability to see what the Father is doing in the unseen world. Every child of God inherits eyes to see what God is doing and ears to hear what He is saying when we are born of the Spirit. We have "entered" into His kingdom and we have the ability to "see" His kingdom manifested in everyday life. We will find what we are looking for! We just need to activate this truth in our lives since it's already a reality. We can live in expectation of seeing and hearing every day because He has united His Spirit to ours. The result is living in greater awareness of the His kingdom all around us through relationship. The key ingredient for a healthy relationship is great communication. God happens to be a great communicator! In the next chapter we will dive deeper into the various ways God communicates to us.

QUESTIONS:

- What are some of the ways that you cultivate intimate connection with the Spirit in your daily life? What would you say is the evidence of your life overflowing with the Spirit's presence?
- What does it look like for you to set your mind on the things of the Spirit? How do you uniquely participate with God in His redemptive plans?
- What is the last thing God spoke to you or showed you? How have you activated your spiritual ears to hear and eyes to see?

DECLARATIONS:

- Sin and death have no power over me. I am free to live in rhythm with the Spirit!
- My life is so full of God that the people around me can't help but encounter Him!
- I was designed to participate with God in His redemptive purposes on the earth!
- God has united His Spirit to my spirit. I have inherited spiritual ears to hear and eyes to see!

ACTIVATIONS:

- Thank God for infusing resurrection life into your spirit through His Spirit. Invite the Holy Spirit to fill you to overflowing with His extravagant love and goodness, and then determine to stay filled daily.
- Write down specific things that help you to set your mind on the things of the Spirit when you start your day. Make it a habit to continue in these things to help you in your focus and sensitivity to His presence and His promptings. He does His part, and we get to do ours.
- Ask the Holy Spirit how you can specifically participate with Him throughout your day. Intentionally look to activate your spirit eyes and ears by getting around others who are hungry for heaven to fill the earth.
- Choose to be a learner and make it an adventure!

CHAPTER ELEVEN

The Language of Heaven

I woke up one afternoon, still groggy from working the night shift the night before. I went into my kitchen to get something to drink and looked out the kitchen window at my backyard. As I was looking back there, I saw a strong gust of wind suddenly blow through the trees. As this gust of wind blew, I was suddenly aware of the presence of God all around me. I instantly had a heightened sense of peace and anticipation rise up inside of me. I stopped what I was doing and asked the Lord what was going on. I then heard Him say, "The winds of change are upon you!" A few months after this encounter, my family and I rented our house out and drove across the country to California for ministry school.

We have learned as a family to flow with the moving and leading of the Spirit, and we have seen the rewards of this laid-down lifestyle. I have sensed and experienced the Spirit's nearness in an increasing measure like this before in both the secret place and in corporate gatherings. I have learned to respond to Him when He draws near like this. We grow in our sensitivity to Him and what He is communicating to us as we respond to the slightest sense of His presence or the slightest whisper. This is the principle of stewardship. He waits to see what we will do with the little things first.

Another time I was at a store to pick up a few things with my wife. I saw a woman in a motorized wheelchair and I had a slight impression and sense in my heart to pray for her. The only thing I was hearing was to tell her God loves her and He is with her. It didn't seem like much, but I have learned to step out with what I have, and then more will come once I step over that line of comfort and safety. I approached her and shared with her what I heard. As I talked with her, she began to cry as she was being deeply touched by God. She had been going through many hardships and challenges with her health and thought God had abandoned her. I re-affirmed that God really loved her and He would never leave or abandon her. She was very encouraged and told me she really needed to hear that because her faith in God was fading. This encounter made her day and changed the way she viewed God. I then prayed for her health, and it was evident that her countenance had drastically changed. Now that is naturally supernatural shopping! I simply obeyed what I heard even though it wasn't much at first. You just never know unless you step out.

Another time I was out to lunch with my pastor and his son in Dayton, Ohio. I was instantly drawn to a girl and a guy standing outside of the restaurant. As I walked passed them, I sensed one of them had a problem with their left knee. In fact, I felt a physical sensation in my left knee that wasn't there minutes earlier. I went back to them and told them that I am learning to hear God's voice and I asked if one of them had a left knee problem. They both said no, so I told them I was learning and got it wrong and just prayed a blessing over them. When I was eating, I told my pastor and his son that I still felt a physical sensation in my knee. I told them it must be for someone else. As we were getting into the truck after lunch, the girl who I approached earlier was trying to get my attention. I got back out of the truck, and she said she needed to apologize to me because she lied to me about not having a left knee problem. She explained how she had been having problems with pain in her left knee for a few weeks. When I said to her, "God showed me someone had a left knee problem," it freaked her out. She explained how she had been recently thinking about God and wondering if He was real and told me this encounter was proof to her that God was real. Wow!

I shared my testimony with her and then prayed for her knee. A couple of days later, her friend called the church and told the pastor's wife that the girl's knee was better now and pain free since I prayed for her. They both wanted to come to our church after that encounter. Come on Jesus!

This is what every follower of Jesus is designed for. It is a beautiful, joint participation and partnership with the Holy Spirit. He is our Friend. I hear some people say, "I can't step out and do that. That's not my gifting or my personality!" My reply to that is everyone can love! You don't have to be an evangelist to demonstrate God to others. The first step to partnering with the Spirit is simply finding ways to love people. Start with what you have, and watch your faith grow. Love is a verb and moves us into action. Let it look like you! Some people ask, "What if I step out and it isn't God?" I ask, "What if it is God?" You will never know unless you step out and take risk. The Holy Spirit empowers us and will be with us. We need to get over our fear of failure and simply be motivated by His radical love.

RHEMA

"Then Jesus was led up by the Spirit into the wilderness to be tempted by the devil. And after fasting forty days and forty nights, He was hungry. And the tempter came and said to Him, "if you are the Son of God, command these stones to become loaves of bread." But He answered, "It is written, "Man shall not live by bread alone, but by every word that comes from the mouth of God" (Matthew 4:1-4).

The first thing the devil attempted to attack was His identity. He tried to get Jesus to prove who He is. Of course Jesus had nothing to prove because His whole value system was found in His connection with His Father. The next thing the devil attacked was the word the Father had just spoken to Him at His baptism. "This is my beloved Son, with whom I am well pleased" (Matthew 3:17). It was no longer a mystery who Jesus was; it had now been publicly announced by His Father. The devil tried to get Jesus to question His identity and purpose by attacking what God had spoken. He did the same thing with Adam and Eve. We lose confidence in our purpose as soon as we question God's word to our heart. Thankfully, Jesus overcame where Adam and Eve did not.

The Greek word for "word" in this passage is "rhema." It is the present and living voice of God. This is different than the written Word of God. This is the personal word God speaks to our heart to sustain and nourish us on the journey. This is what Jesus said was vital for us to rely upon and live by. So the question is, why would we need the personal and current word of God if we already have the written Word of God? It's simple. God created us for relationship. For any relationship to be healthy, there must be ongoing communication. God is a great communicator! This does not mean the written authoritative Word of God is irrelevant. No way! The Bible is absolute truth and will always be. It just means we need to stay current with how God is relationally communicating to us. Staying current with what He is saying to us keeps us fresh and in step with His heartbeat for our lives. It keeps us from getting stuck in a rut in our personal growth and on track with His purposes.

If you haven't already found out, God communicates with us in several different ways. The language of the Spirit is vast and sometimes even unusual. When we sense God speaking to us, it needs to be congruent with Scripture and the nature of God. If it leads us to love God and others, we can be confident that we are hearing from God. It's also important that we are accountable to people in a healthy community of believers.

Within these healthy boundaries we can trust in God's ability to keep us undeceived more than the devil's ability to deceive us. If we ask God for fish, He won't give us a stone. He is a good Father. Some translations of this passage say "every word that proceeds from the mouth of God." To proceed is present tense and means "to always be currently happening." We just need to be tuned in. I have found that God will start speaking to me in different ways in the midst of different situations and seasons in life. If we are not careful, we will live on how He was speaking to us in the last season of life and miss how He is communicating presently. Sometimes we may feel like God is not speaking to us, but it may not be a case of God not speaking to us. It may be that we need to adjust to Him communicating in a way we are not accustomed to. Sometimes God is communicating to us in a way other than His voice. This communication may come by simply sensing His peace or seeing a picture in our mind. This is God communicating with our spirit. God has something fresh from heaven for us every day. It's food and nourishment to our soul, and it's our job to stay tuned in and receptive.

LANGUAGE OF THE SPIRIT

I have found the three most common ways God speaks to me are through Scripture, through creation, and through whispers or slight impressions. I have made it a priority to posture my heart as a hungry learner to receive something fresh from God as I read Scripture. I look for what the Spirit is highlighting or breathing on so that it becomes personal. Through creation, "God's invisible attributes, His eternal power and divine nature can be clearly seen" (Romans 1:20). It's the ability to see God in what He has made (Matthew 5:8). The inner whispers and slight impressions are the ones we can easily miss the most. Many times we dismiss them and say, "That was just me!"

My wife Jenny and I were living in Northern California for a short season, and she had misplaced her capo for her guitar. She thought she had left it in Ohio when we packed our things but wasn't sure. One morning while I was at school, Jenny had this slight impression to go check the glove compartment of our car. As she followed this impression, she found her capo buried in there. What a good Daddy! He cares about a capo just as much as leading us to pray for miracles. She could have missed it, though, because it was one of those slight impressions. How do you know it's God? Risk taking is the key ingredient. We have been given the mind of Christ and we actually discern His mind and His voice much more than we think we do. We just need to go for it so our faith can grow.

The Holy Spirit speaks to us in so many creative ways. Sometimes it's through dreams in the night and visions of various kinds—inner pictures, open visions, etc. I had an open vision of fire across a mountaintop in Hong Kong on a mission trip with YWAM. I didn't even know it was an open vision until the locals told me the next morning that no one ever lights fires on top of the mountain. Ha! God used this open vision to speak very personal things to me that I will never forget. He speaks through other people prophetically, colors, art, music, movies, angelic messengers, signs and wonders, unusual coincidences, etc. This is obviously not an exhaustive list. My goal is to open you up to new ways God may want to communicate to you and lead you by His Spirit.

I have had God confirm things to me in the most unusual ways through His creation. He once confirmed a big decision I made by having two fish swim up to me right after I asked Him to have two fish swim up to me. I was absolutely blown away! He also confirmed a five-day fast he was calling me to by having a flock of birds fly over my head five times. Fun stuff! It's all out of relationship. I am not saying we always need things in the physical to confirm decisions we are making. I'm giving examples of the creative ways God can communicate with us. It's crucial that we stay childlike. For a while I was seeing the time 10:38 a lot on the clock. It began to catch my attention so many times I thought to myself, "Maybe God is trying to tell me something!" I realized He was highlighting Acts 10:38 to me after asking Him about this seeming coincidence. He then made it clear to me that I was in a season of increased awareness of His manifest presence and power upon my life. This gave me insight into something He wanted me to be aware of and to press into during that particular season of my life. These are just a few of the more unusual examples I have. Do whatever works for you to tune into the Holy Spirit, and be expecting Him to communicate to you in new ways every day. I can confidently assure you of one thing—He is not boring!

DISCERNING GOD THROUGH OUR SENSES

"For though by this time you ought to be teachers, you need someone to teach you the first principles of the oracles of God; and you have come to need milk and not solid food. For everyone who partakes only of milk is unskilled in the word of righteousness, for he is a babe. But solid food belongs to those who are full age, that is, those who by reason of use have their senses exercised to discern both good and evil" *(Hebrews 5:12–14 NKJV).*

This passage of scripture tells us that a mark of maturity in the Lord is the ability to discern things in the invisible world through our senses. Notice that it does not talk about discerning right from wrong, but rather "good from evil." This is speaking of spiritual realities and the ability to discern between the works of God and the works of the enemy. This passage also tells us that some are not skilled in "the word of righteousness." What is the word of righteousness? It is the truth and understanding of our nature being restored to what it ought to be in Christ. We have a new creation nature, therefore we now have the ability to discern God and what He is doing with our spirit and our natural senses. We have been made righteous in Christ; therefore our heart, mind, imagination, and natural senses are not evil. The mature in Christ have learned to activate and put to use their ability to discern God through their five natural senses. The Greek word here for "senses" is the word "aistheterion." The meaning is to apprehend, perceive, or to have right judgment. In this context, it is to rightly judge spiritual realities. It is important for us to strengthen our ability to discern God's presence and activity before we try to strengthen our ability to discern the enemy's activity. As we study and experience the genuine, we will more easily discern the counterfeit. The world will see what the Father is doing as we grow in discernment and simply do what we see Him doing. This is what Jesus modeled.

THE FIVE SENSES

The Hebrew understanding is that there is no separation between the natural world and the spiritual world. It is all connected because God is actively involved in all aspects of our lives. In reality, what we call supernatural is actually very natural to God. For King David, there was no separation between the spiritual and natural aspects of his life. It was all connected as he worshiped and loved God with every part of his being. Let's see what the Bible says about our natural five senses: taste, sight (see), smell, touch (or feel), and hearing.

> **Taste and see:** "Oh, taste and see that the Lord is good; blessed is the man who trusts in Him!" (Psalm 34:8).

Smell: "All your garments are scented with myrrh and aloes and cassia, out of the ivory palaces, by which they have made you glad" (Psalm 45:8). This is a description of Jesus the Messiah as our Bridegroom.

Touch or feel: "Oh God, you are my God; early will I seek you; my soul thirsts for you; my flesh longs for you in a dry and thirsty land where there is no water" (Psalm 63:1).

The word "flesh" here is not being used to describe the sinful nature. It is being used to describe David's physical body. This is pretty obvious since the sin nature cannot long for God! David obviously experienced the tangible presence of God to such a degree that he could feel God on his physical body. David was a man who knew God by experience. There are many times when I feel His tangible presence upon my body in times of personal worship or even in times of praying for people. Sometimes I feel Him like heat on my face or my hands. When this happens, I instantly want to know what He is up to. Sometimes He is leading me to pray for someone or He simply wants to enjoy me. The goodness and presence of God can be physically overwhelming at times to the point where it is difficult to remain standing. Even the priests in Solomon's day could not stay standing to minister because of the cloud of God's glory that filled the temple (2 Chronicles 5:14). Sometimes our dignity is on the altar when we experience greater measures of God's presence and glory.

Hearing: "And they heard the sound of the LORD God walking in the garden in the cool of the day …" (Genesis 3:8). What does God sound like? Was it just the rustling of the leaves from His footsteps? I don't think so! I believe the sounds and songs of heaven are being released in the earth as people are tuned in. There is so much more to God than we know or can comprehend. We were designed to experience Him with our whole being so we can participate with Him in demonstrating who He is to the world around us.

THE PURPOSE OF SIGNS AND WONDERS

Some may say not to interpret these verses literally. I understand the importance of being rooted in the truth—to have right beliefs and not to seek an experience. I also understand the Bible is full of people like you and me having dramatic encounters with God. Some of these encounters were very practical and some were very unusual. In times of worship or praying for people, I have seen gold dust appear on people, feathers fall from the air, oil show up on peoples hands, and the physical appearance of angels. I have seen legs grow out, people get out of wheelchairs healed, and the glory of God physically come into a building almost like fog or a mist. I have personally experienced a mysterious fragrance in the air while in the presence of the Lord more than once.

I have also heard many others share testimonies of the same thing. I have encountered a physical wind blow on my body in prayer and have had many tell me they have experienced the same thing. The Hebrew word for "Spirit" is Ruwach. It literally means "wind of heaven." The Spirit of God is like wind. Not just any wind, but the very wind of heaven. Heaven is just waiting to break into our world as we agree with what God is doing. I believe this is in line with the apostolic prayer Jesus gave His disciples in Matthew 6:9–10. This is the "from heaven to earth" perspective.

So the question is, why does God do these things? We are not to seek these signs, but what do we do when it does happen as we are seeking His face? I believe they are signs that keep us in the place of awe and wonder. We are left with only the mind of man when the awe and wonder of God are removed! He is bigger than our understanding. He will never violate Scripture, but He will violate our interpretation of Scripture if it is not in line with His nature and His ways. We can't keep God in the confines of our comprehension. These are signs of God's kingdom breaking into our world. Some things are within our control, but many things are not in our control. God is sovereign, which means He can do anything He wants. It's our job to make room for Him and to discern when He is revealing His nature to us and then respond with adoration and praise. Every sign points to a destination. These things lead us and the world to the Author of life. Every supernatural activity of the Spirit will ultimately glorify the name of Jesus.

Even the Apostle Paul, one of the greatest theologians in history, put a priority on miracles, signs, and wonders (2 Corinthians 12:12). Contained in every sign, wonder, and miracle is a revelation of God Himself. The secrets and mysteries of the kingdom are for those who love God and have eyes to see Him (1 Corinthians 2:9–10). Purity of heart is more than a personal attribute—it is the ability to see God in all things. "Blessed are the pure in heart, for they shall see God" (Matthew 5:8). Those who see Him will be the ones to reveal Him! There is an appetite for the supernatural in every human being on this planet. If the church does not demonstrate to the world the God who wants to encounter them, then the occult and new age movement will continue to feed their starving souls. It's time the world encounters Christians with more than just a theological argument. As Bill Johnson says, "We owe the world an encounter with God."

WISDOM OF THE SPIRIT

"… my speech and my preaching were not with persuasive words of human wisdom, but in demonstration of the Spirit and of power, that your faith should not be in the wisdom of men but in the power of God. However, we speak wisdom among those who are mature, yet not the wisdom of this age, nor of the rulers of this age, who are coming to nothing. 'Eye has not seen, nor ear heard, nor have entered into the heart of man the things which God has prepared for those who love Him. But God has revealed them to us through His Spirit'" (1 Corinthians 2:4–6, 9–10a).

It is clear here that we need both the wisdom and the power of God if we are going to successfully represent King Jesus in every sphere of society. I used to think that being Spirit led meant I didn't use common sense or strategic planning. I thought it had to always be spontaneous if it was coming from the Spirit, but He is both spontaneous and a strategic planner. He shows up like a mighty rushing wind and He downloads wisdom on how to successfully plan a business strategy. He is really powerful and really smart, all at the same time! The wisdom I am talking about of course comes from the Spirit. It is not the wisdom of the world or self-reliance upon our own reasoning. This wisdom is pure and full of good fruit (James 3:13–18). It is for the purpose of revealing the nature of God and to advance His kingdom. The power of God is necessary to reveal the reality of God and His nature to a lost and dying world. Without power demonstrated, we are no different than a good deeds club! The wisdom of God is equally necessary in order to steward the breakthrough that power will bring. We are called to steward our budgets well, do business with integrity, and serve God with excellence. We need to know how to relate to people and how to make great decisions with honor just as much as healing the sick. It takes wisdom to steward a sustained, supernatural environment with lasting fruit. Wisdom will enable us to strategize with God for long-term impact and transformation in society.

The fruit of wisdom is also the evidence of our willingness to be teachable and to be learners. It starts with the posture and attitude of the heart. We can learn from the people around us if we are listening. Wisdom is also the evidence of our dependence upon God. As Paul describes in his letter to the Corinthians, this wisdom is reserved for those who love God. Lovers of God have the inside scoop on what God's plans and strategies are. God reveals His secrets to the humble in heart who maintain a listening ear.

Those who think they are wise according to the standards of this world are actually ignorant when it comes to what matters to God. Solomon is a great example of this. He asked God for wisdom because he knew the task before him was beyond his age and his experience. He had a "listening ear" for the voice of wisdom. As a result, God was glorified through what he built and how he succeeded. He understood what God's strategies were in his generation, and he built into what God was building. He was in harmony with God, at least in the beginning stages of his kingship. We have something to learn from Solomon.

THE FRUIT OF WISDOM

I worked in a distribution center in Ohio for two years, and it was definitely a character-building season for me. I was working the night shift with some pretty rough guys! I always shared the good news with people when

I had opportunity and even had a miracle happen from praying for a guy's infected tooth. He was totally blown away! In the end, though, I knew it was in the way I lived my life day to day that would impact their lives. It was my conviction that they would see Jesus in my attitude, my work ethic, and how I made decisions. I chose to go the extra mile when I could with my clean-up duties and purposed to have a good attitude. There were a few times when I did not represent the character of Jesus well, and I would always go back and apologize for not being honoring in my attitude. My goal was to put the character and power of God on display in my work environment. At the end of my two years, I had an opportunity to share my faith with one of my supervisors and pray for him. He told me that I had impacted him over the last two years because I actually lived what I believed. I was kind of blown away and a little sobered by his statement. I realized how important the process of character building is in our development and ability to authentically represent Jesus to the world.

I believe we are in a time of advancement in the kingdom of God like never before. God is placing His people in strategic places in society to reveal His ways. There is no second-class calling. Let's lean into God with the understanding that no one is meant to be waiting on the sideline. We are all necessary and vital in moving the ball down the field to score for the sake of the kingdom. We need the demonstration of power and the gifts of the Spirit to be in operation or all we have is a nice message. But we also need character and the wisdom of the Spirit to be equally strong in our lives. "Christ the power of God and the wisdom of God" (1 Corinthians 1:24).

QUESTIONS:

- What is God currently saying to you in this season of your life? Could He be communicating with you in a way you are not familiar with?
- In what ways have you experienced God through your natural five senses? Are you hungry for this to increase in your life?
- How are the wisdom and the power of God key to advancing His kingdom in your city? How can you demonstrate both of these realities in your spheres of influence?

DECLARATIONS:

- God is a great communicator. My Father in heaven likes speaking with me!
- I am increasing in a heightened sensitivity to the voice and movement of the Spirit!
- Signs and wonders follow me everywhere I go!
- I am increasing in the wisdom of God. I am a great decision maker!

ACTIVATIONS:

- Spend time in the secret place and "lean into" the heart and mind of God for yourself. Begin to record what He is communicating to you. What are His thoughts toward you?
- Ask Him for wisdom and strategies on how to partner with the Holy Spirit in your spheres of influence. What is your part? Pray into these things and believe for breakthrough. Look for ways to joyfully represent Jesus to your family members, co-workers, or in your neighborhood. Be creative as you seek to demonstrate the wisdom and the power of God through love.

CHAPTER TWELVE

Kingdom Authority

"But that you may know that the Son of Man has power on earth to forgive sins – then He said to the paralytic, Arise, take up your bed, and go to your house. And he arose and departed to his house. Now when the multitudes saw it, they marveled and glorified God, who had given such power to men" *(Matthew 9:6–8).*

The Greek word for "power" here is exousia. It is more accurately translated to be the power of "authority" or "influence." It also means the "power of choice or the liberty of doing as one pleases." As a Son, Jesus had authority to freely represent the nature and ways of His Father as He pleased. He didn't always need a directive from heaven to act and demonstrate the kingdom. I know this seems to be in tension with the very well known verse in John 5:19, "… the Son can do nothing of His own accord, but only what He sees the Father doing. For whatever the Father does, that the Son does likewise." Jesus is the greatest example to us of a life in rhythm with the heartbeat of the Father. The problem is, we use this isolated verse as an unhealthy view on taking steps of faith only if we "feel led" directly from the Lord first. This is not at all what Jesus is communicating in the context of John chapter 5. If you keep reading, you will find John 5:21–23 says, "For as the Father raises the dead and gives them life, so also the Son gives life to whom He will. The Father judges no one, but has given all judgment to the Son, that all may honor the Son, just as they honor the Father." Wait a minute … I thought Jesus only did what He saw the Father doing! Does Jesus only do what He sees His Father doing, or does He give life to whomever He wills? The answer is YES! He does both. In verse 19 Jesus is describing the depth of His oneness with the Father as the foundation for everything He does. He is not saying He can't think for Himself and will only do what His Father orders Him to do. He was always aware of what His Father was doing because He always lived surrendered to His will. They were always one in nature and purpose. Because of this union, Jesus was empowered to give life to whoever He willed to give it to and to judge as He saw fit. He understood the mission of His life, and He understood the authority He was given to reveal what His Father is like as He pleased. His mission and purpose was clear. Jesus did not always need to "feel led" to become the solution to the darkness around Him.

The same is true with us. Grace has restored us to our union with God and placed authority back into our hands. Grace empowers us to exercise the authority given to us for the purpose of destroying the devil's works in people's lives. We get to be the solution to the world around us!

THE REVEALING OF THE CHILDREN OF GOD

It's great when we actually sense the prompting of the Lord or receive a word before we step out. I truly believe we should live expectant for this. We also need to be ready to bring the solution of heaven when we see the opportunity. This is anointing and authority working together. It's both/and, not either/or! We need to be both sensitive to His promptings and also willing to step out with what we already know to be true of who God is and what He is like. I was in Walmart, shopping with my wife one day, and I saw a man with a brace on his leg. I didn't get a word for him or have any directive from heaven. I literally thought to myself, "Let's go and see what happens!" After I introduced myself to him, I prayed for his broken foot and nothing visible happened in the moment. After I prayed, he began to ask me great questions about why God allows natural disasters on the earth. Instead of giving him a theological answer, I just shared the good news of a really good God with him. He was so impacted by what I shared that he ended up praying and receiving Christ with tears rolling down his cheeks right there in the frozen section of Walmart. Amazing!

The crazy thing is, I never heard or received something from God before I approached this man. I understand my mission as a son to partner with God in seeking and saving the lost. I saw a need and stepped out. I didn't need to know it was God's will to heal or save this man. Jesus already paid for his healing and salvation on the cross. I know what my Father is doing and I also know the authority I have been given to share and demonstrate His goodness with people at liberty. We are called to be one with Jesus in nature and purpose just as Jesus was with the Father (John 14:18–21).

This is what all of creation is waiting for—the revealing of the children of God to confidently represent the Father and His kingdom at liberty (Romans 8:19–21). This is the type of leadership Jesus modeled for us as He empowered His disciples and sent them out with authority and the power of influence (Matt 10:1, 7–8). Authority is not based on a feeling or "goose bumps." This authority rests upon us as the children of God whether we are feeling it or not. It is rooted in truth and exercised by faith as we see the need for God's kingdom to break into a situation. We carry this authority and power into every environment and circumstance. The purpose for this authority is to reveal the Father. Our job is to stay surrendered, accountable, and motivated by love. With these priorities in place, we can't go wrong.

CREATED TO RULE WITH GOD

"Then God said, 'Let us make man in Our image, after Our likeness. And let them have dominion over the fish of the sea and over the birds of the heavens and over the livestock and over all the earth and over every creeping thing that creeps on the earth.' So God created man in His own image, in the image of God He created him; male and female He created them. And

God blessed them. And God said to them, 'Be fruitful and mul-
tiply and fill the earth and subdue it, and have dominion over
the fish of the sea and over the birds of the heavens and over
every living thing that moves on the earth'" (Genesis 1:26–28).

The word "dominion" here in the Hebrew language means to rule, take, prevail, or reign. This is the original mission God gave to humankind. We were never originally given a mission to do things <u>for God</u>. Instead we were commissioned to rule <u>with God</u> by expanding the borders of His kingdom (rule and reign) throughout the earth. This is in the context of being in right relationship with God and others. True authority comes out of knowing the Father intimately. It all starts with relationship. Out of relationship, we carry His heart and mission everywhere we go through our lives, joyfully yielded to Him. God wants the whole world to know Him, and He has chosen to reveal Himself through you and me. This is the importance of us learning to live in harmony with His heartbeat in all that we do.

An aspect of the nature of being created to rule with God in the earth involves taking and prevailing. It is in our DNA and job description to take spiritual and physical territory and then occupy that territory for the king-dom of God. In order to see this happen, we need to understand the authority Jesus put back into our hands and the purpose for that authority. Adam and Eve were given authority to have dominion. This included dominion over the devil and his strategies. The second Adam and Eve acted independent of their Father in heaven, they handed over the authority they were given to the devil. Whoever you obey becomes your master! In this case, it was much more of a severe consequence because it had to do with the well-being of the earth and God's purposes for it. The result of Adam and Eve's disobedience was Satan's ability to rule the earth through the sin and rebellion of man's heart. He had influence only because man gave it to him!

The good news is God had a solution. A child would be born and bruise the devil's head and the devil would bruise His heel (Genesis 3:14–15). This child of course is Jesus. The Champion of our salvation! As I explained in chapter four, biblically, the head symbolizes a place of authority. Jesus came to strip the devil of his authority through His triumph on the cross and to take back what Adam and Eve relinquished through their disobedience. He recovered what was lost and put the authority back into the hands of His redeemed people. This is why it is so important for us to understand the greatness of our identity and purpose on this planet. We aren't just destined to go to heaven, we are destined to bring heaven here now! We have been given authority to see transformation in a broken world.

Jesus said to His disciples after he had conquered the grave: "Peace be with you. As the Father has sent me, even so I am sending you" (John 20:21). He sends us in the power of the Spirit with a firm grasp on who God says we are and the purpose of our lives. He sends us with the same kingdom authority and power as Jesus. As it was with Jesus, so it is with us! We have been restored to our original design and mission to rule with God over darkness and to expand the very culture and environment of heaven throughout the earth. This time we will succeed because we are now in Christ and He is in us. We are joined to Him in His victory over sin and death. "But God, who is rich in mercy, because of His great love with which He loved us, even when we were dead in trespasses, made us alive together with Christ (by grace you have been saved), and raised us up together, and made us sit together in the heavenly places in Christ Jesus" (Ephesians 2:4–6). We are presently seated with Jesus in heavenly places and with Him all things are possible! We will succeed because of love. Authority without love becomes abusive. Taking dominion is never to rule over people or to take control. It is to reveal the Father. He is training us to reign with Him through love and with the heart of a servant.

THE HIGH ROAD OF LOVE AND SERVICE

The most excellent way to take dominion of the earth is through bringing love and freedom to people's lives where the devil has ravaged and tormented them. This is what Jesus modeled while He was on the earth. Jesus came to destroy the works of the devil and to set captives free. Everything He did was a demonstration of the Father's nature and will, 100% of the time.

He was absolutely compelled by His Father's love for people in all He did. God is love and so His kingdom is a kingdom of love. Jesus loved and served people well. Even the miracles He performed were all expressions of God's love. Check this example out:

> *"Now a leper came to Him, imploring Him, kneeling down to Him and saying to Him, 'If You are willing, You can make me clean.' Then Jesus, moved with compassion, stretched out His hand and touched him, and said to him, 'I am willing; be cleansed.' As soon as He had spoken, immediately the leprosy left him, and he was cleansed" (Mark 1:40–42).*

Here we see a clear picture of Jesus being moved with compassion to bring the solution from heaven that this man needed. The amazing thing is, Jesus didn't just speak to this man to be healed—He touched him physically. This was probably the first time anyone had touched him since he got the disease. Wow! Jesus demonstrated the Father's love and power to heal this man's body as well as his heart. The works of the devil (shame, disease, rejection, etc.) were destroyed through love in action. This shows us the kingdom value of loving and serving the individual.

My wife and I were leading a group of young people on a two-month mission trip to Guatemala. We spent around nine days up in the mountains in a village. We were sleeping on a concrete slab and taking cold bucket showers, and my wife was seven months pregnant. She is my hero! Every day before we went out, we would spend time in worship and listening to the heartbeat of God as a team. One particular day, we sensed from the Lord to walk around the village and offer to serve in practical ways. So we went out in teams of at least two and helped serve people in their homes with peeling pumpkin seeds, doing laundry and dishes, etc. We even helped a family dig a well in their backyard. People's hearts softened, and they were willing to hear about the love of Christ simply through serving. People's lives were changed. This had a huge impact on my life as well. I am so glad we obeyed the prompting of the Lord that day. I learned the value of simply serving people with no strings attached. This is a clear demonstration of the kingdom of God and how we are called to rule with God through serving others.

God has given us a voice in society as we maintain love and humility. The great commission calls us to be outwardly focused with the heart of King Jesus, whether it is handing someone a bottle of water, cleaning up a sidewalk, or setting a drug addict free through a power encounter with God. Our purpose is to "stop for the one" as Heidi Baker says, and to love our neighborhoods and cities well. Love is a verb—it needs to look like something for people to see and experience.

AUTHORITY OVER DARKNESS

I asked a spiritual father once how I could see more of the supernatural power of God in my life. He responded with passion in his eyes: "Find the darkest places in your city and begin to love on people. You will begin to see God's supernatural power in those places!" This ignited me to action.

I was in the Tenderloin District of San Francisco again on a week-long training and evangelism trip with YWAM. We went out to the streets at night to pass out cups of hot chocolate and to practically show the love of Jesus to hurting people. As we were out one night, we walked past a group of Samoan gang members as they were making fun of us. They asked us sarcastically if we thought we were in Disneyland! I told them we were out praying for people and asked if any of them needed prayer. One of them told me no because it would make him feel bad. Obviously he grew up with some knowledge of God and he knew his lifestyle was not honoring Him.

We continued walking, but I was determined to ask again if the Samoan gang members wanted prayer when we got back to where they were, even though it was a little intimidating. On our way back to the YWAM base, I called out and asked again if any of them wanted prayer. (My team continued on without me. Ha ha!) One guy asked, "What did you say?" So I repeated myself, but I yelled it louder: "Does anybody want prayer?" One of the guys in the gang who was down a block came up and said, "I need prayer!" He never would have heard me if I didn't yell it. God was clearly at work. I noticed a scar on his cheek as he began to share how he was just in a drive-by shooting incident the day before. He explained how a bullet grazed his cheek and he knew God had spared his life! I prayed for him and spent quite a bit of time sharing the gospel with him and his friend. His life was dramatically impacted by that encounter, and so was mine. I understood that night that I was born to be in dark places! We get to join Jesus in rescuing the ones He loves.

The setting and approach may be different, but all of us were designed to be the light of the world in dark places. The Bible calls us "the light of the world." We will shine the most in dark places. Darkness is simply the absence of light. Darkness will continue to rule as long as the children of light do nothing. Whether it's at our workplace, on the mission field, or in our neighborhood, we are abundantly supplied in Christ to confront darkness through love.

EXERCISING DELEGATED AUTHORITY

Authority is not earned or taken. It is given and shared in our union with Christ. We are enabled to exercise authority due to what Christ conquered and overcame on the cross. Living from the victory of the cross enables us take dominion over all of the works of the devil with confidence. Every form of darkness must bow to Jesus when the children of light show up! God is not looking for professionals or those who are refined and have it all together. He is looking to empower sons and daughters who have been captured by His heart to rescue people out of darkness with this glorious gospel of light. Jesus is the light of the world and He lives in us.

My hometown in Washington State is known for its strong new age influence. Some people from out of town had decided to start a new age business called "M.O.M." (an acronym for "Mind Over Matter"). They would meet on Sunday mornings and get people in touch with their "spirit guide." I was a new Christian, but I knew enough to know this was a perversion of the character of Father God and a tactic from the enemy to lead people astray. I was stirred up to do something about it, so I got together with a few other faith-filled friends and we decided to go pray over the building at night. We intentionally prayed at night because we realized our battle was not with people, it was with the demonic spirits behind it.

This was very important for me to learn early on because I could have very easily made people the enemy in my zeal for God. We deal aggressively with darkness as we exercise the authority we have in Christ, but we engage people with love and gentleness, even those who are lost in the darkness of the occult. They are still God's treasures! That night, we prayed all around the building of M.O.M. and declared that it would never get established or take root in any way. We bound the demonic influence attempting to lead people away from their true identity in the Father of lights. Not in our town! A couple of months later, we found out that M.O.M. struggled to establish itself and had to leave our town. Yay God! To be honest, I was a little shocked. I wasn't expecting this to happen like it did even though the Lord had given me a foundation for having authority over darkness when I first got saved.

What I didn't tell you about my salvation experience in chapter one is that a demon physically manifested in my room around five minutes into my being born again. I grabbed my Bible like a weapon and declared, "I rebuke you in Jesus name!" It was all I knew to do, but it worked. The demon instantly left my room. From this experience, I knew there was no junior Holy Spirit working through me and I knew I had authority over darkness. I learned two valuable things from the experience with M.O.M., though. The first thing is the importance of occupying territory when the enemy is driven out. We experienced a breakthrough, but we lacked the wisdom to occupy that building and use it to create a kingdom stronghold in our town. If I could go back, I would have raised the funds to rent or buy that building and would have used it for the Lord's purposes. This was a valuable lesson to learn as I was growing in understanding God's heart to take dominion with the heart and wisdom of King Jesus. The second thing I learned was probably even more important than the first—the kingdom value of being under authority with honor. In many ways, I learned this kingdom value the hard way due to the independent attitude I developed growing up. As we submit to the Father's mission, we are empowered to rule with Him with authority. This is where it is crucial to understand and place value on God's relational government. We must be committed to staying in healthy community in the Body of Christ and honoring the authority God has placed in our lives. If we live isolated and independent from God's structure of authority, we are setting ourselves up to be a casualty of war!

THE VALUE OF ACCOUNTABILITY

It is vital for us to put a high value on being accountable to others in community if we are going to be the cultural change agents God has called us to be. There are no lone rangers in the family of God! I grew up very independent in my upbringing. Years ago I believed the lie that people could not be trusted, and I had to find ways to survive on my own and in my own strength. I carried these lies around like a backpack and brought them right into being a Christian!

It took me quite a few years to really appreciate the people God had placed in my life and to realize I needed them. I remember spending time with God one day, and He said something to me that kind of shook me a little. I heard Him say, "You know, son, a major problem in your life is your pride." He said nicer things to me that day, but this one statement is what I remember the most. I know it seems harsh, but it was exactly what I needed to hear at the time. He spoke it in love and I didn't feel condemned in any way. I look back on my life and I am thankful for my Father's discipline.

> *"For the Lord disciplines the one He loves, and chastises every son whom He receives … If you are left without discipline, in which all have participated, then you are illegitimate children and not sons" (Hebrews 12:6, 8).*

This is different from punishment. Punishment is rooted in anger and is meant to make us pay for the wrong we have done. Discipline is rooted in love and is meant to protect heart connection and to steer us in the right direction. My Father really loves me!

The pride He was speaking to me about that day was my unwillingness to honor authority from the heart and to stay committed to people in community. I didn't see the value and strengths in others around me because I had to prove I was more spiritual and connected to God's heart than anyone else around me. Many times I would be rude with people if I didn't agree with them or if I thought they were complacent in their faith. After God spoke this to me, I began to go through some tough years of learning the value of family, community, and the importance of honoring authority even when I disagreed with them. They were some of the hardest lessons I have ever had to learn! I'm at a place now where I really appreciate the people around me and the wisdom they impart. I have learned to make my top priority protecting heart connection through honor rather than the need to be right. I now know my need for others and I have people that I have given full permission to speak into my life. They give me feedback if I am getting off course with my attitude or the focus of my life. They have taken into account my ability (accountability) and will hold me to the standard of who I am in Christ. Some people may say the Holy Spirit will keep them accountable and they don't need others to do that. Yes, the Holy Spirit keeps us accountable and we rely upon Him completely to lead us into all truth, but we also need others to keep us accountable to the greatness we were designed for. The "I only need God" mentality is actually a recipe for spiritual pride and deception. Why? Because I am left up to myself to discern what is God and what isn't. Nobody was created to live independent like that. I value the different strengths in the body of Christ, and I now realize that a huge part of humility is remaining teachable.

This did not come easy for me, but I do not regret the lessons I needed to go through to learn these core values in my life. The truth is when we were grafted into Christ, we were also grafted into His body. We need each other whether we like it or agree with it or not. We are complete in Christ, but this is not independent of the rest of His people. We are complete in Christ together as a whole body, and we need each other to discern what God is doing in our lives personally, corporately, and in our cities. We are called to build one another up in love. One of the evidences of being filled with the Spirit is our ability to be "submitted to one another in the fear of God" (Ephesians 5:21). The word "submit" here in the Greek means to yield to someone's instruction or advice. It is a "voluntary attitude of giving in, cooperating, assuming responsibility and carrying a burden" (BLB Lexicon). It is a voluntary attitude of being teachable and willing to serve as a responsible team player. No one can demand submission from another. It must be voluntary and decided from a place of trust within the context of relationship. Anything other than submission from relationship and trust is not biblical submission, but control. We desperately need true biblical submission to be modeled in a healthy way in church culture.

UNDER AUTHORITY

God has placed people in the body of Christ to teach us, pastor our hearts, and equip us for kingdom . Maintaining a submitted heart attitude to the leadership God has placed in our lives can be challenging or even frustrating at times, but we need to know it's for our good. God has placed leaders in our lives for a reason. "You only have as much authority as you are willing to be under authority" (Kris Vallotton, *The Supernatural Ways of Royalty*). A good read to understand this biblically is Matthew 8:5–10. This is the test of becoming a true son or daughter in God's house. We cannot afford to try and bypass this important part of our development as world changers.

People in the Bible who left their mark on the world first went through years of preparation and were forged from the fires of character building. We must trust God in these seasons and choose to remain submitted and teachable. I am the only one in control of my heart attitude toward authority, and God cares about the heart above all else. We may even disagree with certain leaders in our lives or feel misunderstood by them at times. This is the opportunity to be honest as courageous communicators without being dishonoring. Disagreeing does not mean we are being un-submitted. We can disagree and keep our honor and submitted (teachable) attitude intact. Secure leaders who value relationship can handle disagreements and are willing to grow from it. If you are under abusive leaders who seek to control and tear you down I would encourage you to get council from others. You may need to align with healthy leaders who seek to empower and build you up. Protecting heart connection in this process is the goal.

This is the high road of commitment to healthy accountability in the family of God. Many people resist the idea of being submitted due to hurts and the fear of being controlled by someone else. The natural reaction to the fear of being controlled is an independent spirit that quickly results in a rebellious attitude. God is healing this by raising up leaders who are learning to be spiritual fathers and mothers in the church, who value family and connection versus control and fear. There are no perfect leaders. Jesus is the only One I have found so far! Even though people let us down, we can still be committed to honoring one another in our weaknesses. God will never fail us! Let's lean into this reality so we can be prepared to bring in a harvest of broken people who are desperate for family.

THE KINGDOM OF HEAVEN IS AT HAND

In 2000, I went on a two-month mission trip to India. Everywhere we went to preach the gospel, people would begin to manifest demons and behave in unusual ways. We were prepared for this in our training before we went, but it was a little crazy at first since we weren't used to it. On one occasion, our team was praying for a woman who was tormented by a demon. She didn't speak any English. As the team was praying for her, a man's voice came out of her mouth in perfect English. Obviously this was not her voice! The voice said, "You are of Western blood. You have no authority over me!" People in the team declared that we had authority because of the blood of Jesus and commanded the demon to come out of the woman. The demon left her and she was set free. The devil will always try to get us to believe that these types of situations are dependent upon our ability, or lack thereof! The kingdom of heaven being at hand or within arm's reach is based on King Jesus Himself being present in full authority and power. He lives inside of us by His Spirit and we have full authority in His name to set captives free. Everywhere we go we can boldly proclaim that the kingdom of heaven is at hand because Jesus is present within us and upon us. We live from the victory of the cross. We must be convinced of this. Some people will argue that the kingdom is not fully here yet and that's why we don't see breakthrough sometimes when we pray. In my opinion, this is a theological excuse for our unbelief due to wrong thinking. Sometimes we look at all of the problems of the world as proof that the kingdom is not fully here. Measuring how much of the kingdom is actually here, or how much of heaven we have access to in this life, should never be based upon the amount of darkness we see around us.

The amount of the kingdom that is here presently is based completely upon the finished works of Christ on the cross and His triumph over death. It is based upon access. We have access to the limitless supply of heaven at any time and in any situation. We could have believed the lie when we were praying for this woman in India. We could have said to ourselves, "Well I guess it's not God's will to set her free at this time!" or "We are lacking in authority" or "It's not the right timing!" The problem with this thinking is it's rooted in lack on our part. We are not called to look at our own lack; we are called to look at the face of our Father. His face reminds us of who we are and what we have access to. He is more then enough for the whole world and then some. There is no shortage in heaven and there is nothing too big for King Jesus! Sure, we are waiting for the fulfillment of His kingdom fully on earth as it is in heaven, but instead of focusing on what is not here yet, let's focus on what we do have access to in the here and now. Let's focus on the solutions we have in Christ rather than how big the problems are around us. This victorious mindset is vital to the apostolic movement God is presently restoring to the church. We are all called to bring heaven to earth in some capacity. As you will learn in the next chapter, you don't need to be an apostle to be a "sent one."

QUESTIONS:

- How have you experienced stepping out and taking risks without a prompting from the Lord or "feeling led" to do so? What was the result?
- How can you be the answer to the darkness around you?
- What does living in healthy community and being under authority mean to you? Has that been a positive or negative experience for you? How can you increase the value of this in your life?

DECLARATIONS:

- I was created to rule with God through love and service!
- Darkness is afraid of me. Everywhere I go captives are set free!
- I am designed to be in community. I was re-born into a family!
- The kingdom of God is present everywhere I go!

ACTIVATIONS:

- Take the time to think through where you thrive the most in community and healthy relationships. Which relationships challenge you and sharpen you to grow and excel in the greatness of God? Focus on building these relationships. Look for ways to increase your level of honor through serving others in healthy community. Take a risk and choose accountability with people who will spur you on to greatness.
- Adopt a dark place in your city that's in need of the love and power of Jesus. Begin to pray and get God's heart for the treasures (people) living there. As you pray, begin to dream and imagine with the Holy Spirit about how you can creatively influence that place with the kingdom of God. As my friend Steve Bowen says, "Begin from where you are with what you have." Go ahead and take a risk and see how God comes through. It might be giving food to a homeless person, releasing healing to someone who is sick, encouraging someone who needs it, taking time to pray for a co-worker, etc. Have fun and get others to join you as you make a difference with the love of Jesus!

CHAPTER THIRTEEN

Apostolic Mission

My wife and I pioneered a training and equipping school in Springfield, Ohio in 2011. It was the first equipping school of its kind in the region, and we were very excited to pioneer this with God. We named it Kingdom Culture School of the Supernatural with the intent of equipping and empowering an army of passionate lovers of Jesus who would change our city. Although we would not consider ourselves apostles, the Lord had clearly given us an apostolic vision with this school. We wanted to see society transformed and we knew the strategy was not a new program or an event—the strategy of heaven is people. We understood the school was only a vehicle in order to equip and empower people to carry kingdom culture into their spheres of influence. This is God's plan A to see long-lasting transformation in our cities, regions, and nations.

These are the core foundational beliefs we built this ministry upon:

- God is good 100% of the time. He is always smiling over us and always with us!
- We are a new creation. We live from our new identity in Christ as delighted-in sons and daughters. We presently have full access to all that Jesus paid for with His blood.

- Our mission is to bring heaven to earth! God empowers us with authority over darkness and has anointed us as world changers in our spheres of influence.
- We are a family. We have a commitment to community and living a life of love and honor.

With these core beliefs in place, our students and interns began to understand that a school does not make a person a world changer, the God of the universe living inside of them makes them a world changer! Believing truth about who God is and who we are in Christ is where we begin to live out our assignment as change agents in any environment. We would always say to our students, "If what we are teaching you and equipping you with does not work outside of this building, then we are wasting our time!" We refused to settle for just a successful school—we wanted kingdom transformation coming through transformed people. This has always been the goal.

In our very first Kingdom Culture orientation, we had two girls who were not registered as students show up for prayer. They told us, "We were told to come to Kingdom Culture if we needed healing." We were a little taken back by that statement because this was our very first school orientation and there were already rumors about us in the city. That's when I knew the vision was much bigger than a school. One of the girls had scoliosis and one leg was shorter than the other, which caused pain in her back. One of my staff and some students jumped all over this opportunity. They had her sit down in a chair and checked her legs. Sure enough, one leg was shorter than the other so they held her legs out and commanded the short leg to grow out. Instantly the leg grew out and matched the other leg. She got up and her back pain was completely gone. This caused everyone's faith level to skyrocket! They were now ready to take on her scoliosis. I went out to put some chairs away while they continued praying for her. All of a sudden, I heard yelling and cheering while I was in the other room. I quickly went into the room where they were praying for her and asked what was going on. They explained to me that they started commanding her spine to straighten up, and as they were praying they saw her spine begin to straighten so drastically that they could see her shirt moving around as her spine moved. The room was ecstatic! This was an amazing start to Kingdom Culture being launched. God was making a clear statement to me. This movement will not come through the superstars and the people behind the pulpit; it will come through every day people who are passionate about Jesus and His kingdom. It will come through people who are committed to passionately pursue the heart of Jesus and are willing to take risk together in the context of family and community.

HEAVEN'S MISSION

The great commission is an apostolic mission from heaven. It was given to the first apostles by the Lord Himself. The Greek meaning of the word "apostle" is "sent one." "As the Father has sent me, I also send you" (John 20:21). You don't have to be appointed as an apostle to be a "sent one" with the mission of heaven. Every single one of us are called to "go into all the world" in some capacity and be light in dark places. We are all called to be agents of transformation whether that takes place in our family, workplace, university, among the poor, or in a foreign country. I believe one of the ways God is presently restoring apostolic mission and purpose to the church is through apostolic leaders. When you come under apostolic leadership, you begin to function in an apostolic grace and anointing. Apostolic grace and anointing gives us the ability to see the world through God's eyes—the whole world as a mission field! The mission is to see every sphere of society transformed.

> "... declared to be the Son of God in power according to the Spirit of holiness by His resurrection from the dead, Jesus Christ our Lord, through whom we have received grace and apostleship to bring about the obedience of faith for the sake of His name among all the nations ..." (Romans 1:4–5).

Paul received grace (empowerment) and apostleship (anointing) to call people among the nations to the obedience of faith in Christ. This is the description of his God-given assignment. Grace was the supernatural empowerment of Christ Himself upon Paul's life to accomplish that assignment. Paul's apostleship was more than just a title—it was an aspect of Christ's nature and leadership imparted to him as a gift to the body.

> *"And when He had called His twelve disciples to Him, He gave them power (authority) over unclean spirits, to cast them out, and to heal all kinds of sickness and all kinds of disease ... And as you go, preach saying, 'The kingdom of heaven is at hand. Heal the sick, cleanse the lepers, raise the dead, and cast out demons. Freely you have received, freely give'"* (Matthew 10:1, 7–8).

Before Jesus sent the twelve out to go and freely give what they had freely received, He first called them to Himself. The fact that He first called them to Himself reveals the importance of time getting to know His heart. He then empowered them with authority from this place of friendship to accomplish what He was sending them to do. Authority is never taken. It is always given for a specific assignment and purpose. He sent them out with clear instructions for the proclamation and demonstration of His kingdom. Grace empowers us not only into the greatness of our identity, but also into the greatness of our apostolic purpose. Grace is a Person. The more we pursue Jesus out of pure love for Him, the more we will naturally be moved by His heart for the world around us. It is impossible to be with Him and not be moved by His kindness and passion for an orphaned world. The more we are with Him, the more we carry inside of us what's inside of Him. Grace is not self-centered in nature. It's not focused on what we can get away with or how we can stretch the boundaries of our rights and freedom. Grace restores us to who we were originally created to be and empowers us to God's original purpose for all of humanity—to co-labor with Him in expanding the borders of His kingdom throughout the earth. This is the heartbeat of the apostolic mission of heaven given to the church. This mission is what apostolic leaders are called to both demonstrate and empower the body of Christ within the context of family.

MISSIONAL FAMILY

"The more heaven comes to earth, the more it will look like family" (Kimberly Johnson). This is the heartbeat of heaven. This is the direction God is going, and He is inviting us to follow Him into exploring what it looks like to have family on earth as it is in heaven. In order for this to happen, I believe we need to get past a misconception in understanding apostolic leadership. Some believe that if we are going to develop an apostolic culture in the church, then we will prioritize the presence of God and mission over family. There has been a comparison and maybe even a divide between Apostolic church communities and Pastoral communities. The idea for some is apostles are driven by the mission of heaven and aren't geared toward caring for people's needs and developing a sense of family in the church. Pastors, on the other hand, prioritize family and the needs of the people. I believe there is some truth to this that helps in understanding the differences between the anointing and priorities of apostles and pastors, and helps us understand how both need each other. Pastors gather and shepherd people to health, while apostles empower and send people out to change the world. Both are highly valuable in the kingdom. The idea that apostles will not prioritize family, though, is just not true from a biblical perspective. To understand this better, we need to take a look at God's original mission given to Adam and Eve.

When God first commissioned Adam and Eve to have dominion of all the earth, the first thing He did was bless them and command them to be fruitful and to multiply. In terms we understand, He told them to have lots of babies and grow the family (Genesis 1:26–28). This was God's plan to fill the earth with people who would be in harmony with His heart and His purpose. The understanding was the dominion of God would expand throughout the earth through family. God's plan was to spend enough relational time with Adam and Eve in the Garden until they truly knew Him and understood the greatness of their identity and purpose. They would in turn raise their children up in this same environment. This is the relational government of God on earth. In this model, each succeeding generation can go further in taking ground and advancing the kingdom of God rather than having to start from square one. God has always been a Father and His heart has always been family from the beginning.

When the church was birthed and led by the original apostles, they shared everything. They broke bread together and valued togetherness and heart connection as a family. They met in larger gathering places to worship, as well as in homes. Out of this place of connection and love founded in the Holy Spirit, they also participated in a shared mission to proclaim and demonstrate the gospel of the kingdom with signs following (Acts 2:42–47). The believers in the book of Acts "continued steadfastly in the apostles doctrine and fellowship." The grace upon apostolic leaders is to equip the church to fulfill the mission of heaven as a family. They are called to establish heaven's culture and governmental structure in a way that is conducive to a powerful and healthy community of Christ followers who are making a lasting impact on the world around them. The church is both a family and an army. We are first a family, though, because the first miracle prioritized in heaven is the orphan becoming a child of God. This is the top priority of heaven. Papa God first sent His Son to rescue an orphaned world in order to populate heaven with many sons and daughters. His plan from the beginning has always been to build a family who would become a force for transformation in society.

Even the Apostle Paul identified himself as a spiritual father to others (Galatians 4:19–20, 1 Timothy 1:18–19). God's government is absolutely relational, and it's about time the world experiences the true heart of the Father through the church functioning as a family. The church is meant to be a place where people feel connected and empowered as world changers, all at the same time. Children excel and grow naturally in a healthy home environment where they can express themselves and experiment. Likewise, the church is designed to be a safe environment where the sons and daughters can express themselves and take risk with honor in order to excel and grow. They are then empowered from this safe environment to represent Jesus to the world. A broken and orphaned world is longing for this to be modeled. They need a church with the priority of relational wholeness and vision for societal transformation. We are called to be a missional family who reveals the true nature of a good Father. To align with heaven, apostolic leaders must prioritize family.

UNDERSTANDING APOSTLES

Apostles can be the most misunderstood out of the five equipping gifts mentioned by Paul in Ephesians 4:11. We understand that prophets prophesy, evangelists evangelize, pastors shepherd, and teachers teach. They also equip and activate others to do the same. But what do apostles do?

To understand apostles and the anointing they function in, we need to look at the apostolic prayer and mission Jesus gave to the original apostles. He told them to pray this: "Your kingdom come, Your will be done, on earth as it is in heaven" (Matthew 6:10). This is an apostolic prayer that is focused on earth looking like heaven. Apostles are primarily focused on the environment of heaven and making that a reality here on earth. Apostles focus on what heaven is doing, and then they join their value system and purpose in life to that heavenly vision. Apostles are big visionaries with a huge desire to influence culture with the kingdom of God. They will never be satisfied with the status quo or with safe church growth plans. They burn to see heaven manifested in the earth!

Jesus also gave the original apostles a clear mission: To "go ... and make disciples of all nations" and to "go into all the world and proclaim the gospel" (Matthew 28:19, Mark 16:15). This is an apostolic mission that is focused on being a force for change in all the world. The early apostles did not just impact synagogues or the church world, they "turned the world upside down" (Acts 17:6). Notice how it says "into all the world." The gospel the apostles proclaimed and demonstrated influenced every realm of society. This is what God is calling the church back to.

John Wesley and George Whitefield are a great example of apostolic leadership. They preached out in the open fields as the first Great Awakening sparked in the 1700s. This awakening touched all of society to the point where most of the favorite bar songs were turned into worship songs! The same can be said of Saint Patrick during the fifth century. Known as "The Apostle of Ireland," he received wisdom and strategies from heaven on how to reach the barbarians of Ireland through their own culture. He planted monastic communities who did not separate themselves from the world, but rather engaged the world with the culture of heaven. Saint Patrick and his monastic communities ended up discipling the whole nation of Ireland through storytelling, music, creativity, and the power of God. Apostolic leaders are graced to see whole cities and nations transformed by the good news of Jesus. The Apostle Paul is a great example of this. He was a "sent one" with a clear assignment from heaven. He was both a missionary who preached the gospel with signs and wonders, and he was a church planter. He was both a visionary and a builder who built upon the foundation of Jesus Christ. Apostles always blaze trails into new territory. They can tend to face increased measures of resistance and persecution at times, due to shaking up the status quo of church culture and the bent toward pioneering new territory in various arenas of society. This helps us have a better understanding and appreciation for the grace and function of apostles.

APOSTOLIC PRIORITIES

Apostles raise up apostolic-minded people who are geared toward cultural transformation. They also empower others to pioneer and take new territory for the kingdom of God. This can be expressed through church planting, but not always. It can also look like pioneering new business strategies or new creative expressions in the entertainment industry. Apostolic people are some of the best entrepreneurs and innovators in society. Apostolic-minded people tend to take more risks in a world that is constantly changing. This takes creativity, wisdom, and thinking outside of the box. The kingdom of God is always increasing and advancing in an apostolic environment. The vision will be so big that the supernatural power of God will be absolutely necessary to fulfill it! This is much like the great commission given to the first apostles—power was necessary for them to accomplish their heavenly assignment. Left to their own ability, fulfilling their mission would've been impossible! The gospel without power is not an option for true apostolic leaders. Miracles, signs, and wonders are expected and become the normal Christian life. A person who claims to be apostolic but does not demonstrate the power of God is not truly functioning in an authentic apostolic anointing. Listen to what the Apostle Paul says about this priority:

"But I will come to you soon, if the Lord wills, and I shall find out, not the words of those who are arrogant but their power. For the kingdom of God does not consist in words but in power" (1 Corinthians 4:19–20).

"I have become foolish; you yourselves compelled me, actually I should have been commended by you, for in no respect was I inferior to the most eminent apostles, even though I am a nobody. The signs of a true apostle were performed among you with all perseverance, by signs and wonders and miracles" (2 Corinthians 12:12).

Demonstration of power for the original apostles was both normal and necessary to engage the world they lived in as witnesses of the resurrection of Jesus. The world needed an encounter with the living God, or darkness would continue to rule. The same is still true today! Apostles are given blueprints from heaven to advance the kingdom of God into new territory with wisdom and power. Their assignment is to bring the culture of heaven "into all the world" and equip and empower others to do the same. They are very much regionally and globally minded. Pioneering apostolic leaders are usually more concerned with what God is doing than creating a safe and cozy environment. The impossible must be invaded!

We absolutely need all five of the equipping gifts listed in Ephesians 4, but it is my opinion that prophets, evangelists, pastors, and teachers will function best when connected to apostolic leaders or apostolic ministries. Why? Because apostles keep the "big picture" mission of heaven toward earth at the forefront. The other four can fully thrive in their anointing when connected to apostolic leadership because it's all for the purpose of fulfilling the great commission. Evangelists will bring in the harvest, and pastors will shepherd them to health in the family. Teachers will disciple them with the Word, and prophets will equip them with eyes to see the Father and ears to hear what He is saying. This is all so they can join the army of world changers! Equally important is the apostle's need for the other four equipping gifts. All five are the 100% expression of who Christ is and His government increasing in the earth. This does not mean every local church community needs an apostle leading. It just means we need to think regionally as leaders and join together with heaven's purposes and priorities. All five equipping gifts must learn to work together and value the different graces and expressions of Christ in each other, whether we are in the same church community or not. Each one is an expression of Christ. This is key for the kingdom to advance. The revelation of Jesus in the earth is, and always will be, the focal point!

A BIG MINDSET SHIFT

There is a major shift happening in the church. We are beginning to understand that the church cannot fulfill the great commission without apostolic grace and authority. For many years, the church has been primarily focused on gathering to a building. Many times we find ourselves caught in the rut of "doing church" better for the purpose of church growth, instead of listening to the heart of God for our communities. I believe this is all changing at this time in history. God is restoring apostolic and prophetic voices in order to restore the apostolic anointing and mindset to the church. This is the mindset needed to be outwardly focused with the mission of God's heart to disciple whole cities and nations. He has strategies on how we can touch society with the gospel if we will take the time to seek Him and listen.

I truly believe that without apostolic leadership and mission, society goes untouched by the gospel of the kingdom for the most part. This is why we see cities with hundreds of churches on every corner, and yet society is not being transformed. It takes apostolic anointing to see society touched by the reality of heaven in a sustainable way. It takes the wisdom and the power of God. Apostolic leaders are not superstars by any means. Their call is to equip and empower others with God's heart and purpose. The purpose for apostles, prophets, evangelists, pastors and teachers is to equip the whole body for the works of ministry (Ephesians 4:11–16).

Ministry is being redefined in the church. Ministry is not just for people who are called to serve full time in church leadership or on a local church staff. Ministry, or kingdom service, comes out of who we are in Christ. It comes out of the overflow of a life filled with God. We are all anointed and called to continue the ministry of Jesus. Instead of a consumer mentality where people just "go to church" to be served by the pastoral staff, people will come to serve and to be equipped to impact the world around them. The idea of just going to church is over! Sunday morning spectator Christianity doesn't work. God is not breathing on it! The reason why we gather and assemble together is because we are the church! We are united by the Spirit of Christ who resides within us. A building does not define who we are. God defines who we are. We are the children of God and we are family. We're a community of Christ followers. I believe we need to rethink and redefine the purpose for why we gather as believers. We are not called to create an outdated, irrelevant subculture within a building; we are called to engage society with the revolutionary gospel of grace!

EMPOWERED BY LOVE

One of the things that excites me about ministry being re-defined is the fact that many are embracing their God-given assignment to bring kingdom impact into their work place, schools, city, and through various creative expressions and talents. There is no second-class calling or anointing. This burns in the heart of God! He wants all of His kids to live with the mission to bring heaven to earth wherever He has given us influence. People are coming into family and experiencing God's radical love. The result is fear is getting driven out of people's lives and they are getting activated into lifestyle Christianity. Experiencing God's extravagant love transforms us from orphan to son and daughter, and from fearful to bold. Our lives are forever changed in His love!

In our Kingdom Culture school, we had a 17-year-old girl still in high school as one of our students. The thought of praying for other kids at her high school totally freaked her out! As our school went on, she grew in her confidence as a royal daughter of the King through life-changing encounters with Papa God. She began to grasp her authority and knew God would show up and do extraordinary things when she prayed. She grew in confidence because of the environment of the school and the emphasis on practicing by taking risk in a safe place.

It wasn't long before she began stepping out and praying for others at her high school. It all started when she prayed for another girl at her locker. The girl was complaining about neck pain, and after she prayed the girl's pain went away. They were both absolutely blown away! She was so bold that when a teacher asked what they were doing, she simply replied, "We are praying!" He apologized for interrupting and went on his way. After she experienced her first breakthrough, she became an unstoppable force in her school. She had testimonies every week our ministry school met. As a leader, this is what it's all about for me. This young girl and many others like her is why I am doing what I'm doing. God's intentions are that His presence (anointing) would rest upon all of His people. This is the priesthood of all believers. We are all anointed with a purpose. His plan for transformation in the different spheres of society has always been people, not new and improved systems and better church growth programs. The driving force is the love of Christ compelling us to be a living, breathing, missional family, full of the transforming power of Jesus. This is God's idea for the gospel of the kingdom to invade every realm of society. He plans on doing it through you and me!

THE VALUE AND PURPOSE OF FAVOR

"Jesus grew in stature and in favor with God and man" (Luke 2:52).

The fact that Jesus grew and excelled in favor both with God and with man tells us that we too can grow and excel in favor. The word "favor" in the Greek has the same root meaning as grace. Favor is completely unearned, and yet it is something we can increase and grow in. Favor is the benefit and reward of being a child of God. The more we grow in confidence as His child, the more we understand the favor He has placed on our lives. The key to increasing in favor is stewarding the measure He has already given us.

God equally loves every person, but not everyone is stewarding the same measure of favor. This is not an issue of competition or of who is more valued, but rather a means to further the kingdom of God. It's important to keep our priorities right as we excel in favor. The more favor we have with God and man, the more responsibility we have to represent the heart of King Jesus by serving and empowering others. I believe Jesus wants to give His people favor with man in every realm of society. He wants to give us a voice and a place of influence just like Joseph had with Pharaoh. As we learn faithfulness and stewardship in little things, He will entrust us with greater influence.

Joseph learned to be faithful in the dungeon before he was raised up at the right hand of the Pharaoh. This is a key component for our development and growth in the Lord and our ability to impact society. If you desire a crop to harvest, God will give you a seed and see what you do with it. If you desire a million dollars, He will give you a thousand dollars and see what you do with it to multiply it. The kingdom principles of faithfulness and stewardship are not to work for or earn favor and influence. They exist so our character will be equal to the measure of favor He has given us. Navigating the test of trials and hardships is one thing. Navigating the test of increased greatness and favor can be equally, if not more revealing, of what motivates our hearts. God will not give us more than we can handle, but He will bring us into new territory to see how we handle it. Our job in this is to keep our priorities aligned with His heart and purposes. Lovers of God keep their affections in the right place!

One of the ways we will be tested to see how we will handle our own favor is how we respond to others being favored and promoted. Will we respond with jealousy like Joseph's brothers did? Or will we celebrate? This will ultimately determine how much favor we can handle, and how we will steward it for the purposes of His kingdom. Orphans can never celebrate someone else's increase because orphans live with a deep-rooted sense of lack: "If someone else receives blessing, then there is not enough for me!" This mentality will always lead us into the need to fight for our place of significance. This is a sure path to heartache and frustration. As cherished sons and daughters, we know that there is always more than enough in our Father's house. This mentality of abundance will lead us to the freedom of celebrating others when they receive breakthrough and favor. Our time will come as we remain faithful to our assignment in the season God has us in. The big test will come when someone gets a breakthrough or a promotion in the exact area we have been desiring and praying into. Paul tells us in 1 Corinthians 12:25 to "suffer with those who are suffering and rejoice with those who are honored."

Personally I think we have struggled more in rejoicing with those who are honored because of religious mindsets rooted in false humility. We can quickly assume that if someone is honored or promoted, they are arrogant or self-seeking. We need to overcome this and rightly steward favor if we are going to influence society with the kingdom of God in a healthy way. Wisdom is key in this process, as it was with Joseph, Daniel, and many others in history whom God exalted for His purposes. This is very important if we are to understand the apostolic grace and mission of the church. Our mission is to bring the transforming culture of the kingdom into all the world. For some, this will look like being in places of great position and influence. Many will be raised up with innovative ideas and out-of-the-box strategies from heaven. Not everyone is called to just influence church culture. I believe we are beginning to learn how to lead and shepherd people with this level of influence and favor without insecurity. We need everyone in the game if we are going to see an army of empowered world changers who are equipped to see entire nations discipled.

QUESTIONS:

- What has your understanding been of the apostolic mission of the church? What in this chapter was new for you? What is your part in this mission being fulfilled?
- Are there any apostolic churches or ministries in your city or region? Are you connected to them relationally?
- What sphere of society have you been called to influence (business, government, media, arts and entertainment, education, family, or religion)? How do you uniquely bring kingdom impact into this arena?

DECLARATIONS:

- I am joined to my Father's mission to bring heaven to earth!
- I am a part of something bigger than I know! I am being prepared for great things.
- I am stepping out and taking more risks this year than I did last year!
- I am increasing in favor with God and man.

ACTIVATIONS:

- Join with others who are passionate about the expansion of God's kingdom and develop a personal mission statement. Ask God to give you specifics on how you can uniquely bring the culture of heaven into your neighborhood, workplace, etc. Let love and honor toward people be the motivator.
- Go on a declaration rampage about your mission statement and who you are called to influence. Ask God for specific promises from His Word you can agree with. This is a victorious mindset that agrees with heaven's truth rather than focusing on all of the world's problems. Record what you are believing for, and then journal the results as you get breakthrough. You are God's solution and plan A to make a difference!

CHAPTER FOURTEEN

Empowered as World Changers

I am so hopeful and excited about how God has set the stage for a great harvest and work of transformation to happen on a regional and a global scale. People all over the world are growing in an appetite for the supernatural power of God, even in the Western world! Some would say this is a trick from the devil to lead many astray into the new age movement and the occult. I actually disagree. I think it is a set up for the church to rise up and put the love and power of Jesus on display so a hungry world gets the real thing. The empowering grace of God is being abundantly poured out on a generation of radical lovers of Jesus to answer the heart cry of an orphaned world—the cry for the reality of God to be experienced in a world full of darkness.

I took my son, Judah, with me to get our hair cut not too long ago. The lady who was cutting his hair asked me what I did for a living, so I told her I was a pastor. She then began to open up to me about a dream she had a couple of weeks prior. She explained how she was driving near her old workplace in her dream and noticed a bunch of people out of their cars with much commotion and chaos. She got out of her car to find out what was going on and noticed everyone was looking up to the sky. As she looked up, she could see a figure coming down toward everyone. As everyone saw the figure, they all got on their knees and began to cry out, "Jesus! Jesus!" She knew it was Jesus coming to the earth, so she thought she should probably get on her knees along with everyone else. After she got on her knees, the dream ended.

I was blown away by what she shared with me! I asked her what this dream meant to her. She pretty much said she wanted to understand what it meant to get her life right with the Lord. I told her I had nothing but good news for her! I shared the good news of the death and resurrection of Jesus and parts of my own testimony with her. The crazy thing is she had very little exposure to the gospel or church culture. She had already believed in Jesus, though, because of the dream. She just needed me to explain it to her so she could make a conscious choice to follow Him. After that, I asked her if I could pray for her to be filled with the Holy Spirit. She was open and ready to receive prayer right in front of her co-workers without any fear or shame.

As I prayed for her, I sensed the presence of the Spirit come into the room. I asked her what she experienced while I was praying. She said she could feel a breeze blowing on her and that she could breathe easily. I told her that God had come to live inside of her and would be with her forever. The breeze she was experiencing was the Holy Spirit. She was so happy!

I shared this encounter with my evangelist friend who explained to me how people in the 1970s during the Jesus Movement would have dreams about Jesus coming to the earth just like this woman had. They would get saved as a result. I began to ask the Lord what He was saying through this. After talking to others, I began to get some insight. I believe we are presently in one of the greatest harvests of people getting saved the earth has ever seen. Past movements of God will only be a glimpse of what is to come. It will not be in just one location or through one person's ministry, but in various locations and through many ministry expressions throughout the earth. This harvest has already started in some parts of the world where people are being saved by the thousands. It is also going to hit the United States again, and Jesus is going to be the focus of this movement. This is a movement involving the whole Body of Christ. He is raising up an army of young and old all over the earth. We need everyone in the game. All of us were created to reveal the Father's goodness through good works.

CREATED FOR GOOD WORKS

"For we are His workmanship, created in Christ Jesus for good works, which God prepared beforehand that we should walk in them" (Ephesians 2:10).

We are His work of art—a masterpiece that points to the kindness and goodness of the great Artist. Our lives are a testimony of God's amazing grace. He took us from death to life and from darkness to light. Your life shines with the splendor of your Creator! Not only are we His workmanship, but we were also created for good works. These works are to put on display the greatness of our God. The works we were designed for are in Christ Jesus. These are good works, not dead works! Good works are empowered by grace and fueled by faith. Good works reveal the nature of

God through sons and daughters who live and work from acceptance and approval. Dead works are empowered by self-performance and fueled by the need for approval, acceptance, and praise from man! The difference between the two is an issue of motivation and mindsets.

Yes, we are called to be the children of God, but we are also called to do the works of God. We get to join God in what He is doing in the earth. People need to see the works of God through our lives. This is how God designed us. "Grace is not apposed to effort, it is opposed to earning. Earning is an attitude. Effort is an action" (Dallas Willard, *The Great Omission*). Just because a person is very active in accomplishing a lot in the kingdom does not mean he or she is stuck in performance or religious activity. We are called to judge people by their fruit, not by their motives. In my experience, joy is usually a visible fruit in the lives of those who are accomplishing good works fueled by the love of God. People working for approval are usually disgruntled and joy impaired! God knows the motives of the heart better than we do.

It is becoming popular to have a grace theology and strongly frown upon using the word "work" or the idea of putting any effort into anything. I've heard it said, "We don't need to do anything because Jesus already did it all!" This is a partially true statement. Jesus removed the sin nature to restore us back to unbroken union with Papa God. He took back the keys

REVOLUTIONIZED *by* GRACE

of the kingdom from the devil and is now seated at the right hand of God with all authority. He didn't stop there, though. He gave us the keys of the kingdom and commissioned us to go and bring the good news into all the world. From this perspective, we have much to accomplish in advancing His kingdom in the earth. We are called to join God and put effort into the things He cares about. We will find God's wind in our sails as we join His mission to bring heaven to earth. At times we will even need to contend and go after things to see kingdom breakthrough we are desiring in our families, cities, or nations. We need strategies and wisdom from the Lord to see breakthrough in society, and sometimes we need to persevere in those strategies. I am not saying it needs to be difficult to see breakthrough or that a place is "too hard spiritually." I have seen breakthroughs come quickly and easily, and other times it takes enduring faith as we stand firm in His promises. Even when we endure and persevere in faith to see transformation in our cities, it is done from a place of rest and partnership with God. The sacrifice of Jesus is enough provision for the whole world. Nothing is too difficult for God.

God is raising up a last-days army of passionate lovers who know how to lie down in His presence and receive, and they also know how to persevere in the battle until breakthrough comes. He's raising up an army of faith-filled believers who don't mind grabbing a shovel to dig deep when work needs to be done. This is good works from a place of enjoyable union with Christ. Joining God in what He is doing then becomes a delight and a privilege.

FULLY EQUIPPED

"As the Father has sent Me, I also send you" (John 20:21).

Our Father would never ask us to do something or go somewhere that He did not intend on fully equipping us for. Jesus was sent with full confidence in His identity, significance, security, and purpose in the Father. Jesus understood with conviction the greatness of His identity and purpose. This was most likely revealed to Him by the Father in many ways, but at His baptism, it is clearly revealed to us. "And when Jesus was baptized, immediately He went up from the water, and behold, the heavens were opened to Him, and He saw the Spirit of God descending like a dove and coming to rest on Him; and behold, a voice from heaven said, 'This is My beloved Son, with whom I am well pleased'" (Matthew 3:16–17). Jesus lived in the abundance of His Father's provision, empowerment, and most importantly, His delight and approval. His life was an open heaven. He didn't lack anything! As a beloved Son, He lived from abundance.

Jesus lived from the reality of His Father's full approval and backing in everything He did. He was fully equipped with everything He needed to successfully fulfill what He was sent to do. The Father empowered Him with authority to bring His kingdom reality and rule everywhere He went. The same is true of us! Jesus sends us in the same way He was sent by the Father. We have the same abundant resources and spiritual equipment at our disposal as Jesus had to successfully fulfill what we are sent to do.

> *"And Jesus came and said to them, 'All authority in heaven and on earth has been given to Me. Go therefore and make disciples of all nations, baptizing them in the name of the Father and of the Son and of the Holy Spirit, teaching them to observe all that I have commanded you. And behold, I am with you always, to the end of the age'" (Matthew 28:18–20).*

Our mission is so much bigger than our natural abilities. It takes childlike faith and trust in the Father's ability to do the impossible in and through us just like He did through Jesus. There are two powerful aspects found in this Great Commission: The call to make disciples of individuals and the call to disciple whole nations. The Father makes sure we are equipped to bring individuals into the family to find healing and wholeness, and He also equips us to disciple and influence whole nations with His love, wisdom, and power. We can't have one without the other. We need to work together in the Body of Christ as a family and as a force for transformation. Transformed people end up transforming the world around them! We are heaven's access to earth. All of us are equipped to bring the freedom and healing of heaven to earth.

GOSPEL OF DIVINE WHOLENESS

I was on staff at a YWAM base in Northern California, and during a summer youth camp there, I noticed a young girl on crutches with a wrap around her knee. The Lord whispered in my ear to go pray for her. My wife Jenny and I went up to her and introduced ourselves. We asked her questions about her knee to find out what was going on. We found out her boyfriend threw her down and her knee was injured as a result. It was pretty intense!

We asked her if we could pray for her, and she was very open to it. As we were praying, I saw a picture in my mind of me suddenly straightening her knee out and declaring, "Be healed." After I told her what I saw, she explained how her doctor tried to do that exact same thing the day before, and it hurt her so badly that she hit the doctor. I thought maybe God was setting me up to get knocked out by this girl! She reluctantly allowed me do it after sharing with her that I believed God would do exactly what He showed me in the picture. I decided to test it out and move her knee a little bit before I straightened it out all the way. It was so stiff! To be honest I was a little scared, but I went for it anyways. I suddenly straightened her very stiff knee out and declared, "Be healed!" Afterward she instantly began to cry. I asked her if she was crying because it hurt. I honestly wasn't sure! She explained that she wasn't crying because it hurt, but because it didn't hurt. I think she was shocked that it worked. She then got up and began to bend her knee and put weight on it. She said with tears, "I couldn't do that before!" She was completely healed on the spot! She walked away carrying her crutches and was totally blown away by the goodness of God.

The most amazing thing for me was what I discovered about God after this miracle happened. I learned that there is a revelation of the nature of God contained in every miracle. We just need to look for Him in everything He does. I realized that not only did her knee get healed, but her heart got healed too. The Father restored trust and safety in her life where it was violated by her boyfriend. She could trust her Father in heaven, knowing the truth that He would never do anything to hurt her. The Father's heart was put on display and the works of the devil were destroyed—that's a good day in the kingdom! God desires to heal the whole person when He encounters them. Christ paid for us to live in divine wholeness spiritually, emotionally, mentally, physically, and relationally. He died to make us whole in every aspect of our lives, and we have the privilege of bringing this good news to broken people as He has brought healing into our broken lives. His desire is for all of humankind to be made whole, and He has given us His love and power to demonstrate this.

The world needs to know God is not mad and that He is in the business of restoring lives. He was broken on the cross so the whole world could be made whole. The healing ministry of Jesus is continuing today, both within the church and out in the marketplace. I truly believe that the ministry of healing in and through the church is meant to be just as consistent as the ministry of reconciliation. Forgiveness and healing are the children's bread! Both of these aspects of Christ flow in the same river from God's throne. They work hand in hand (Psalm 103:1–3).

SMEARED WITH HIS PRESENCE

"How God anointed Jesus of Nazareth with the Holy Spirit and with power. He went about doing good and healing all who were oppressed by the devil, for God was with Him" (Acts 10:38).

The Greek meaning for "anointed" is to be smeared or made shiny. Jesus was smeared with the Holy Spirit and with power. He didn't just receive an anointing from the Holy Spirit. Anointed "with" means He was literally smeared with the Holy Spirit Himself. Just think about that for a minute … What are the implications of having the Holy Spirit Himself smeared all over you? As it was with Jesus, so it is with us! This is available to each one of us. We were born to carry the tangible presence of God upon us. This is how we change the spiritual climate wherever we go. This is how Peter's shadow healed people. He was so smeared with the Holy Spirit that even his shadow carried the anointing of God's presence.

Jesus was also smeared and made shiny with miracle power. It is absolutely crucial for the Spirit to live on the inside of us in order to become a child of God and to display good fruit. It is just as crucial to be carriers of the tangible presence and power of the Holy Spirit upon us if we are going to bring kingdom transformation to the world around us. Jesus needed power to complete His purpose, and the disciples needed power to fulfill the Great Commission. It would be completely arrogant of us to think we don't need something that Jesus and the apostles needed!

Anointing has to do with purpose. God doesn't anoint us so we can go around telling people how shiny we are! He anoints us to reveal what He is like to the world around us. He does this in the unique way that each one of us expresses His heart. He is in us for the sake of relationship; He is upon us for the sake of the world! Without the supernatural ability of God, we are left to our own abilities and ideas. The Holy Spirit in us and upon us causes the best version of who we are to shine. God is best glorified when the best of who we are comes out. His presence upon us causes the greatest creativity to be expressed through our lives.

When David was bringing the ark of God back into Jerusalem, he made a mistake and it cost a man his life and a three-month delay in returning the ark. He tried to return the ark on a cart. During those three months, David discovered something that changed his life. He discovered that the ark was to be carried upon the shoulders of priests. This was the way God chose to transport the ark. The ark symbolizes the very presence and glory of God. God has never desired for His presence and glory to rest upon man-made programs and systems (this is what the cart symbolizes). He has always desired to rest upon the shoulders of priests. Priests minister to God's heart as worshipers and on behalf of the people as intercessors. Through the blood of Jesus, all of us have become priests to our God (Revelation 1:5–6). As a child of God, you have been set apart to love God as a worshiper and to be smeared with His tangible presence and power upon you to change the world. This is what Jesus told His apostles to wait for in Jerusalem before they even attempted to make disciples of all nations. This baptism of the Spirit, smeared upon the apostles with power, comes by promise and is still available to us today. Without this smearing of the Spirit and power upon us, we will not be able to fulfill our mission on the earth. God is looking for people He can trust with His power. People who will steward His power with humility and won't seek to be exalted by men. In fact, He wants to trust this kind of anointing and power to a whole generation!

THE POWER OF PEACE

It was a late night as my friend and I were heading back to my home after an amazing time in the glory of God at our ministry school. I decided to drive the back way home through the neighborhood we had adopted as a school. As we were coming up to a gas station, I heard the Lord whisper to me, "Pull into this gas station." I was tired and really didn't want to stop. To be honest, I was totally going to ignore what He said and keep driving. Ouch! As we were about to pass by the gas station, my friend said, "Pull over in this gas station! There's a guy and a girl fighting!" When I pulled into the parking lot, my friend jumped out and walked right into the middle of this guy and girl fighting. The girl was yelling at her boyfriend and hitting him. My friend was concerned that the boyfriend was going to start hitting back! He went right up to them and asked them if they needed any help. Right when he asked them this, they stopped fighting and actually walked away from each other. The guy came over with my friend to where I was, and we talked to him for a little bit. After that, we began to pray for him and he calmed down. Then the girl came over to us, and we prophesied life and value over her. God touched both of them with His presence that night. My friend was fearless because of God's presence and peace that was saturated all over him. God's presence makes us fearless! This is the power of peace in a world of conflict and chaos. Biblical peace is not the absence of conflict, it's the presence of King Jesus! His peace brings well-being into any environment. The kingdom of God is righteousness and peace and joy in the Holy Spirit (Romans 14:17). We get to release peace (total well-being) everywhere we go as carriers of God's presence and power. We are ambassadors of an unseen world and we represent the Prince of Peace. The world is desperate for the peace we carry!

> *"For to us a child is born, to us a Son is given; and the government shall be upon His shoulder, and His name shall be called Wonderful Counselor, Mighty God, Everlasting Father, Prince of Peace. Of the increase of His government and of peace there will be no end ..." (Isaiah 9:6–7a).*

THE POWER OF PRAYER – RELEASING HEAVEN!

"Our Father in heaven, hallowed be Your name. Your king-dom come. Your will be done on earth as it is in heaven"
(Matthew 6:9–10).

One of the most amazing things to me is how God invites us to join Him in releasing His kingdom and His will to be a reality on earth, just as it is in heaven. He wouldn't invite us into this prayer and declaration unless it was possible. That means our prayers, coupled with faith, will actually change things in the world around us by releasing the reality of heaven. We can change the outcome of individuals, neighborhoods, cities, and nations through agreeing with God in prayer.

Jesus modeled prayer that was not begging God or striving to convince Him to be good or merciful. He is already good and merciful. Prayer does not change who God is, it changes us and the world around us! This happens by simply positioning our hearts to agree with what He is doing from heaven to earth. This approach to life completely changes our perspective. Praying from heaven to earth brings us into the right focus because we begin to see the world through God's eyes. From this perspective, we begin to pray in response to what God is doing rather than praying in reaction to what the devil is doing. It doesn't take any faith to point out the problems of the world. It does take childlike faith to believe with God for the solution. This is what we need in our day and time. So many people are filled with fear and the mindset that things are only getting worse. As faith-filled believers, we have the opportunity to declare to others the goodness of God and the solutions He has.

Prayer is a relational invitation to join with God in His purposes for our world. It starts with "Our Father in heaven," which concludes that relationship must be the foundation our prayer life is built upon. Initially, prayer is meant to get to know God, His heart, His will, and to experience His nature to be good in all things. The more we get to know Him and learn to enjoy Him, the more we will understand His will and begin to simply agree with Him in our prayers and declarations for others. The more you spend time with God, the more you will be outwardly focused and compassionate for others because God is a lover of all humanity. It is interesting, though, that Jesus did not tell us to pray "My Father," but rather "Our Father." Obviously we are all called to cultivate a personal prayer life, but there is power when we pray together as the family of God in agreement with heaven. It's in agreement with who God is and what He is doing that cultivates unity. Paul called it "maintaining the unity of the Spirit in the bond of peace" (Ephesians 4:1–3). Consequently, unity is not created or maintained through doctrinal agreement. It is maintained through the bond of peace because we already have "the unity of the Spirit." We just need to maintain it through love and honor. That way we can agree together for His kingdom to come in increasing measures into a darkened world.

The way we treat each other will either put fuel on what the Spirit is doing, or it will quench what He is doing. Disunity and offense in the body of Christ actually hinders the will of God from being realized. It is important for every believer to grow in personal kingdom intercession, and equally important is growth in corporate kingdom intercession. Intercession is not a spiritual gift for only a select few. As Christ followers, we are all called to live lives of intercession. We are all empowered to agree with God in declaring the release of His kingdom and will at any time or in any circumstance. We have been given authority to demonstrate what heaven is like. Whether we are agreeing with God's heart for others from a distance or in direct contact, our declarations change spiritual atmospheres and destroy darkness. This is in the DNA of every child of God!

THE GIFT OF FAITH

One of the greatest gifts we can ask for as we are learning to agree with God is the gift of faith (1 Corinthians 12:9). Faith gives our hearts eyes to see into the unseen world where the Father is ruling and reigning. If you can see with childlike eyes of faith what the Father is doing, then you can join Him. The key is knowing Him. The more we get to know Him, the more we know what His will is. This gives us the confidence we need to represent Him to others. The key is also thinking like God. This is the mind of Christ. Our ability to think like God gives us the ability to approach specific situations the way He would approach them. In essence, asking God for the gift of faith is asking for ears to hear and eyes to see. Stepping into what we are seeing and hearing is the key to unlocking greater levels of faith in our lives.

When we were running our Kingdom Culture school, we adopted a pretty rough neighborhood in Springfield, Ohio. We led teams into that neighborhood every Saturday to love on people in practical ways. One Saturday, I saw a man digging a big tree stump in his side yard. Different family members and friends were out there, watching him dig, so we struck up a conversation with them. I found out as I was talking with the man that he had injured his lower back and was in a lot of pain. He didn't think he could finish digging the stump out due to the pain. The gift of faith rose up in me as I sensed the Lord wanting to heal him.

I told him that if I prayed, he would get healed right there on the spot. I then asked all of his family and friends if they wanted to see a miracle. Of course they all said, "Yes!" I asked his daughter if she had ever seen a miracle. She told me she had never seen a miracle and seemed a little skeptical. I asked her if she was ready to see God heal her dad's back. She reluctantly said, "Yes." On a scale of 1–10, (10 being the worst) the man said his pain was a 10. I prayed a short prayer and asked him to check his back out. He bent over several times and twisted around with no pain at all! He tried to find the pain, but he could not find it. Come on, Jesus! Everyone was shocked and in amazement. We were then able to talk to them more about Jesus and gave prophetic words to the daughter. She got rocked by the love of God. That's a great day in the kingdom!

The gift of faith is actually the faith of Christ in operation through our lives. This is where we see things from heaven's perspective much clearer for a specific time or event. This then requires us to act upon what we are hearing, seeing, or sensing. Heaven manifested in the earth is as simple as stopping to love on an individual or receiving strategic downloads from God to transform your business or your city. It's simply demonstrating the love, power, and wisdom of God in our everyday life. The more we take action with what we are hearing and what we are seeing, the more we will see the world around us transformed.

GLORIFYING GOD THROUGH ANSWERED PRAYER

It's time for us to step into impossibilities with childlike faith in the One who loves to make Himself famous through our answered prayers. Answered prayer is fruit that glorifies God (John 15:7–8). He isn't glorified through unanswered prayer. Unanswered prayer points to me. It points to God when people see what He has done supernaturally on my behalf. Answered prayer is part of our birthright as the children of God.

It is imperative to pray from the reality of His acceptance and approval. We must pray from a place of abundance! Living with an orphan mindset means living from a place of lack. Orphans are busy working hard at getting what belongs to them because there is not enough to go around. This is a description of an attitude and spirit of entitlement. We can't pray with faith for heaven to break into the issues of our world if we pray with a mindset of lack.

Beloved sons and daughters pray with extraordinary faith because they know there is no shortage with God. They pray with the solution in mind, not how big the problem is! The question then becomes how much of heaven can we see manifested in this life? I don't know the answer to that, but I do know Jesus didn't give us a limit. I believe this is an invitation to see how much of heaven we can believe for. His resources and the solutions He has are limitless. We just need to tap into who God is and pray from the knowledge of His revealed will. This gives us the confidence that we will see the answered prayer because it is in agreement with Him (1 John 5:14–15). He truly is an extravagantly good Father!

Read the lyrics of this song and let it stir faith in you:

> "Is it true today that when people pray, cloudless skies will break, Kings and Queens will shake? Yes, it's true! And I believe it. I'm living for You. Is it true today that when people pray we'll see dead men rise and the blind set free? Yes, it's true! And I believe it. I'm living for You.
>
> I'm gonna be a history maker in this land. I'm gonna be a speaker of truth to all mankind. I'm gonna stand. I'm gonna run into Your arms. Into Your arms again.

Well, it's true today that when people stand, with the fire of God and the truth in hand, we'll see miracles, we'll see angels sing, we'll see broken hearts making history. Yes, it's true! And I believe it. We're living for you." – "History maker" by Martin Smith

Heaven wants to break into every aspect of your life—your finances, your relationships, your coworkers, your city! Heaven looks like righteousness, peace, and joy. It looks like love and forgiveness in action. It looks like power to set captives free and to perform miracles. It looks like Jesus! Let's make this song our declaration and the reality of what our lives look like in Christ.

CHRIST-CENTERED GOSPEL

"The Gospel is centered in God's Son, a descendant of David by human genealogy and patently marked out as the Son of God by the power of that Spirit of holiness which raised Him to life again from the dead. He is our Lord, Jesus Christ, from whom we received grace and our commission in His name to forward obedience to the faith in all nations" (Romans 1:3–5 Phillips Translation).

I was speaking on a Sunday morning at a church in Richmond, Indiana about the goodness and presence of God. I shared a few testimonies of how I have encountered Him first hand and how my life was forever changed as a result. After the service, an older woman called me over to talk to her. She was honest with me at the start of our conversation of how she was skeptical of experiencing the goodness of God. She explained how she was apart of a Jehovah's Witness church for years and had to get out of it because of the harsh rules and regulations. She had never experienced the goodness of God and she was desperate for His love! As I was listening to her, this thought went through my mind: "She has only known the false Jesus. Has she ever received the real Jesus?" I instantly knew this was wisdom from the Spirit. I explained to her that what she had experienced for years was a false Jesus. I then began to describe the real Jesus to her. She came to tears because she desperately wanted a loving Savior who would gladly accept her and forgive her. I then asked her if she had ever received the real Jesus. She said no. I asked her if she wanted to, and with her consent, I led her in a prayer of salvation. It went something like this: "Father, thank You for sending Your Son to die for me. I believe in my heart He rose from the dead. I renounce the false Jesus (wrong spirit) and declare you are not a part of my life anymore! I receive the real Jesus. I receive Your love and Your forgiveness for all my sins. I declare You are the Lord of my life. I ask You to fill me with the Holy Spirit. Amen!"

I asked her how she felt after we prayed, and she said it was like a burden or a weight was lifted off of her. She was filled with peace. I welcomed her to the family and she was so happy. Yay God! She needed to know that she didn't need to jump through hoops. She simply needed pure love. She needed the real Jesus!

After this encounter, I was stirred in my heart with so much gratitude for the Person of Jesus. He is so good! He Himself is the good news. He is the greatest gift to all of humanity. I believe a wave of fresh revelation of the Person of Jesus is going to hit the church and splash out into society. Not necessarily a new revelation, but the truth of the beauty and majesty of who He is as our reigning King. We need the real Jesus who loves and forgives and encounters our hearts! He is so full of pure love and His power is available to instantaneously set people free from lies and oppression. He alone is the cure for the human condition. He is the answer to the heart cry of every heart on this planet. The Spirit of God is bringing us back to the simplicity of the gospel and how it is still "the power of God for salvation to everyone who believes" (Romans 1:16).

His grace is still transforming lives, and Jesus is still the focal point and champion of this salvation. Let's come back to the "sincere and pure devotion to Christ" and then lead others to do the same (2 Corinthians 11:3). He is the desire of the nations, and the Father has preserved the best wine for last. The beauty and majesty of His Son will be put on display for all to see, and the earth will once again be in awe and wonder of who He is. We will once again be intoxicated by His pure love and presence. He alone satisfies our deepest desires. His love alone makes us fearless in a darkened world.

The greatest privilege we have is to join God in His pursuit of a broken and orphaned world. This is the heartbeat of every expression of evangelism. We get to join Him in the passion of His heart and reveal the greatest gift to all of humanity. This is the revolutionary gospel of grace that both transforms and empowers—Christ Himself. The whole world is longing for what you and I have tasted and seen. Let's join with heaven and declare what we have seen and heard so the whole world can intimately know the Father and the Son as we do.

> *"That which was from the beginning, which we have heard, which we have seen with our eyes, which we looked upon and have touched with our hands, concerning the word of life – the life was made manifest, and we have seen it, and testify to it and proclaim to you the eternal life, which was with the Father and was made manifest to us – that which we have seen and heard we proclaim also to you, so that you too may have fellowship with us; and indeed our fellowship is with the Father and with his Son Jesus Christ"* (1 John 1:1–3).

QUESTIONS:

- What does it look like for you personally to be empowered by grace into good works that glorify the Father? How do you uniquely express His kindness to the world around you?
- What has the Father specifically equipped you with as a world changer? Have you ever thought of yourself as a world changer? How can you bring healing and peace into your sphere of influence?
- Do you believe that your prayers have the power to release heaven? What would it look like for heaven to be released in your neighborhood or your city? How has God already been glorified through your answered prayers?

DECLARATIONS:

- I have been transformed and empowered by grace to change history!
- I am anointed (smeared) with the Holy Spirit and power. I have a purpose!
- My prayers bring heaven to earth. I carry the atmosphere of heaven wherever I go!
- God is for me and empowers me to succeed. I am a world changer!

ACTIVATIONS:

- Start a prayer-walking group in your neighborhood or adopt another neighborhood in your city. Ask God for specific things to pray for—specific prayer targets. Don't focus on what the devil is doing, but rather focus on what God is doing. Record the changes you see over time as you pray and show the love of God in practical ways.
- Find other world changers who are passionate for the heart of God and for His kingdom to be advanced in your city. Begin to pray together and creatively think of how you can reach out to your city together with the love and power of Jesus. Start with committing to loving on at least one person a week as a lifestyle and reaching out to your city in some way with a group of fellow Christ followers once a month. Let these things be the catalyst that activates you into a missional lifestyle.

ABOUT THE AUTHOR

Stephen Bell and his wife, Jenny, live in Springfield, Ohio with their four amazing children – Jasmine, Judah, Savannah, and Scarlett. Stephen and Jenny served on staff at Youth With A Mission in Chico, California for seven years. During their time with YWAM they had the privilege of ministering the hope of the gospel in several nations. Stephen's life is marked by the supernatural, and he is passionate about activating people in their identity and purpose as beloved sons and daughters of God. He has a heart to mobilize the Body of Christ with an apostolic mission to bring heaven into every realm of society. Stephen is currently serving as the Associate Leader at RiverSong Church. He is regularly a guest speaker in local churches and ministry schools. If you would like to get in touch with him or invite him to speak at your church or event, you can contact him at revolutionizedbygrace@gmail.com